DESERT POTLUCK

A COOKBOOK
PRESENTED BY

All Saints' Episcopal Church

and

Day School

A FIREBIRD PRESS BOOK

PELICAN PUBLISHING COMPANY
Gretna 1998

Manufactured in the United States of America

Published by Pelican Publishing Company, Inc.
1000 Burmaster Street, Gretna, Louisiana 70053
ISBN 1-56554-667-9

PREFACE

A veritable cornucopia of tasty delights is herein joyfully offered to you in this culinary masterpiece prepared by the ladies of All Saints' Episcopal Church and Day School.

Through your support of this cookbook, All Saints' Day School will be able to continue its longstanding policy of providing tuition assistance to all youngsters, regardless of race, creed, color, or national origin, who meet our admissions standards and are in need of financial support. Sixty-two percent of our student population comes to us from non-parish families and we count this ministry our primary outreach mission.

Further, your support of this cookbook will enable All Saints' Church to both expand its ministry to youth and to reach out more fully into the community and provide food, clothing, housing, transportation and emergency assistance to those in need.

And so, as you feast your eyes on the magnificent drawings of Phoenix artist Mary DeLoyht Arendt, and you treat your palate to the delights of these recipes, please know that others are being fed in mind, body and spirit through your generosity.

Bon Appetit!

Carl G. Carlozzi, D.Min.
Rector/Headmaster

EXECUTIVE COMMITTEE

Kay Allen
Betty Heisley
Suzan Makaus
Donna Hahn
Nancy Hume
Robin Rasciner

ASSISTED BY

Bonnie Ashton
Cindy Gilbert
Susan Mark
Claire Stone
Sandy Brandau
Joan Gorczyk
Francey Potter
Brenda Vermeire

The Committee thanks the members and friends of the Church and Day School for their enthusiastic support of DESERT POTLUCK. We believe the variety and beauty of the Arizona desert is reflected in this collection of recipes and illustrations.

TABLE OF CONTENTS

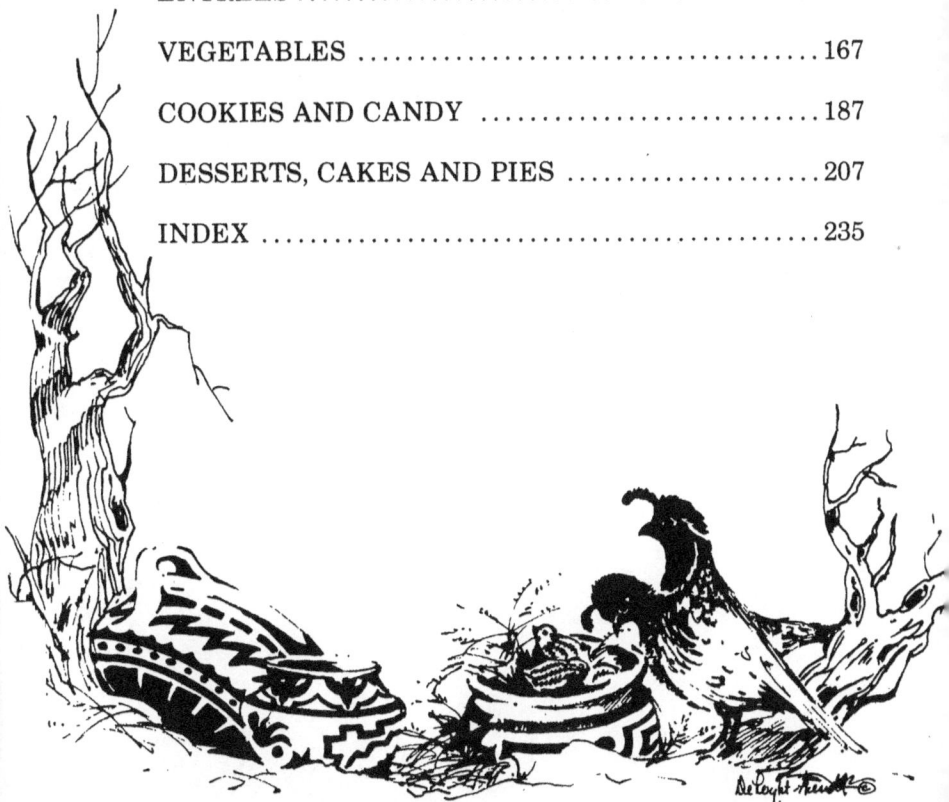

appetizers and beverages

BEAN DIP

1 10½-ounce can bean dip
8 ounces sour cream
8 ounces cream cheese
½ package dry taco seasoning
1 cup grated Monterey Jack cheese
8¼-ounce can refried beans, optional

Combine bean dip, sour cream, cream cheese and taco seasoning in an oven-proof casserole. Refried beans may be added if desired for additional color and texture. Top with cheese and bake at 325° for 20 minutes.

Makes 4 cups

CHIPPED BEEF DIP

Use as a dip or spread on crackers.

8 ounces cream cheese, softened
2 Tablespoons milk
1 2½-ounce jar dried beef, finely chopped
2 teaspoons instant onions
2 teaspoons chopped green pepper or green olives
½ cup sour cream
¼ cup chopped walnuts or pecans
1 teaspoon horseradish (optional)

Combine all ingredients, mixing well, and place in baking dish. Bake 15 minutes at 350°.

Serve hot or cold. This keeps well.

Serves 8 to 10.

SOMBRERO DIP

Serve warm with tortilla chips.

1 pound ground beef
¼ cup chopped onion
¼ cup extra hot catsup
2 teaspoons chili powder
½ teaspoon salt
2 15-ounce cans red kidney beans, pureed
1 cup shredded longhorn cheese
½ cup chopped green onions

Brown meat and ¼ cup chopped onion in skillet.

Stir in catsup, chili powder and salt, mixing well. Blend in kidney beans and heat through.

Place mixture in chafing dish and garnish with a ring of grated cheese and a ring of green onions.

Makes 5 cups

DATE RUMAKI

Looks familiar from the outside, a surprise on the inside!

¾ cup brown sugar
½ cup water
⅓ cup lemon juice
¼ cup cider vinegar
1 teaspoon grated orange rind
½ teaspoon cinnamon
¼ teaspoon nutmeg
⅛ teaspoon salt
1 pound pitted dates
12 slices bacon, cut in thirds

Combine all ingredients except dates and bacon in a saucepan and boil until sugar dissolves, then simmer 5 minutes.

Transfer mixture to a glass bowl and marinate the dates, in the refrigerator, at least 24 hours, stirring occasionally.

Drain dates and wrap in bacon; secure with a toothpick. Broil for 15 minutes and cool 10 minutes before serving.

Makes about
3 dozen

CAVIAR POTATOES

Red potatoes, very small
Butter
Freshly grated Parmesan or Swiss cheese
Sour cream
Caviar

Bake very small red potatoes; cut in half and scoop out most of potato. Dry out skins in oven. Spread butter on inside of skins and sprinkle with cheese. Just before serving, warm skins; set out with bowl of sour cream and one of caviar. To eat, place dab of sour cream on skin, then dab of caviar.

MEXICAN BEAN PIZZA

Delicious served with tortilla chips or corn chips.

1 17½-ounce can refried beans
1 cup grated Cheddar cheese
1 6-ounce can frozen avocado dip
2 tomatoes, diced
1 bunch green onion, sliced
1 2¼-ounce can ripe olives
1 pint sour cream

In an 8″ square baking dish, spread beans and top with grated cheese. Heat in a 350° oven 10 to 15 minutes or until cheese is melted. Cool.

Spread with avocado dip and sprinkle with tomatoes, green onions and ripe olives. Ice with sour cream and chill until ready to serve.

Serves
6 to 8

COCKTAIL SPINACH BALLS

This attractive hors d'oeuvre can be made up to 6 weeks ahead and frozen.

- ½ cup sesame seeds
- 2 10-ounce packages frozen, chopped spinach
- 2 cups garlic or herb-seasoned croutons
- 1 cup grated Parmesan cheese
- 4 eggs, lightly beaten
- ¾ cup unsalted butter, softened
- ½ teaspoon ground white pepper
- ¼ teaspoon nutmeg

Heat medium-sized skillet over medium heat; add sesame seeds. Cook, stirring constantly, until seeds are golden, 2 to 3 minutes.

Cook spinach according to directions. Drain in a sieve, pressing with back of spoon to remove as much moisture as possible.

Grind croutons into fine crumbs in blender or processor. Place in bowl and add spinach, cheese, eggs, butter, pepper and nutmeg. Mix thoroughly. Shape into small balls (about 1 rounded teaspoon each) and roll lightly in sesame seeds.

Freeze in single layer on waxed paper-lined baking sheets. Transfer to airtight container or freezer bags.

To bake, place balls on ungreased cookie sheet in a 350° oven for 10-15 minutes.

Makes about 50.

JOSEPHINAS

1 4-ounce can diced green chiles
¼ pound butter, softened
1 cup mayonnaise
½ pound grated Monterey Jack cheese
2 loaves French bread, thinly sliced

Mix chiles, butter, mayonnaise, and cheese until well blended. Spread amply on bread rounds, making sure to cover well. Place on ungreased cookie sheet in a pre-heated broiler for 5 to 10 minutes.

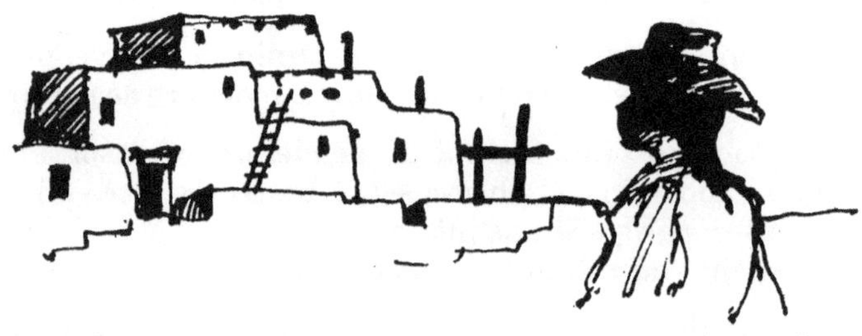

GREEN CHILI SQUARES

1 4-ounce can chopped green chiles, drained
1 pound grated sharp Cheddar cheese
6 eggs, beaten well

Spread the green chiles in the bottom of a buttered 8″ x 8″ baking pan. Sprinkle the cheese over the chiles and pour the eggs over all. Bake uncovered at 350° until firm, about 30 minutes.

Cut into 1″ squares. Serve warm.

Makes 64 squares.

PASTA PATÉ

1 cup cooked pasta (fetticini, egg noodles, elbow macaroni, etc.)
8 ounces cream cheese, softened
¼ cup grated Cheddar cheese
½ cup sour cream
3 Tablespoons finely chopped onion
3 Tablespoons finely chopped green pepper
2 Tablespoons chopped pimiento
¼ teaspoon cayenne

Cook pasta according to instructions on package for al dente; if using long, thin pasta, break pasta sticks into thirds before cooking. Drain, rinse with cold water and set aside.

Combine cheeses and remaining ingredients. Gently fold pasta into cheese mixture, taking care to distribute noodles evenly throughout.

Lightly grease small loaf pan, 6″ x 5″ x 2″. Place pasta-cheese mixture in pan. Cover and chill until firm, at least 1 hour. Unmold: Run edge of knife between pasta and pan; invert and rap smartly on board.

Place paté on cheese board or small serving platter. Serve with pumpernickel or onion-flavored crackers.

CHILI FINGER QUICHE

½ cup margarine
10 eggs
½ cup flour
1 teaspoon baking powder
¼ teaspoon salt
2 4-ounce cans diced green chiles
1 3½-ounce can hot chili peppers, drained and diced
1 pound grated sharp Cheddar cheese
2 cups small curd cottage cheese

Melt margarine over low heat in 9x13-inch cake pan. Set aside.

In large bowl beat eggs slightly.

Sift together dry ingredients, add to egg mixture and mix thoroughly. Add chiles and cheese and mix thoroughly. Pour into baking pan and mix until the melted margarine is thoroughly distributed in egg mixture.

Bake at 350° about 1 hour. Test with knife for doneness.

Makes approximately 48 1-inch pieces.

May be made ahead and refrigerated or frozen, as it retains moistness and flavor. Reheat for serving.

UBIQUITOUS CRAB

6 ounces crabmeat, canned or frozen
¾ cup mayonnaise
6 ounces cream cheese, softened
½ pound grated sharp Cheddar cheese
1 onion, minced
2 hard cooked eggs, minced
¼ teaspoon dry mustard
½ teaspoon paprika
Freshly ground pepper

Mix crabmeat with mayonnaise until smooth; add remaining ingredients and mix well. Refrigerate.

Serve as appetizer with Triscuits or party rye.

DENISE'S SHRIMP MOLD

This can be served as a first course or as a salad.

1 10¾-ounce can condensed cream of mushroom soup
6 ounces cream cheese
¾ cup mayonnaise
1 Tablespoon gelatin, dissolved in 3 Tablespoons water
1 medium onion, grated
1 cup diced celery
2 4½-ounce cans broken shrimp

Heat soup, cream cheese and mayonnaise until warm and ingredients are blended.

Add gelatin and remaining ingredients. Pour into a 5-cup mold and refrigerate 24 hours.

MARINATED GREEN CHILES

Use as topping for cream cheese to be served on crackers.

1 cup vinegar
½ cup sugar
2 Tablespoons dill seed
1 Tablespoon mustard seed
4 6-ounce cans diced green chiles
2 cloves garlic

Simmer vinegar, sugar, dill and mustard seeds 10 minutes.

In a 1 quart jar, place green chiles and garlic. Pour hot liquid over, cover and refrigerate.

Keeps indefinitely in refrigerator.

ROYAL MUSHROOMS

Can be done day before, or frozen, and then baked and served.

24 to 30 large mushroom caps
⅓ cup finely chopped green onion
3 Tablespoons butter
1 10½-ounce package frozen chopped spinach, defrosted and strained
¾ cup minced ham
1 cup sour cream
Salt and pepper to taste

In heavy skillet, sauté onions in butter. Add spinach. Toss and cook over low heat 3 to 4 minutes. Remove from heat. Stir in ham and sour cream. Season. Sprinkle inside of mushroom cap with salt. Spoon mixture in. Place in buttered pan and dot tops with butter for extra richness, if preferred.

Bake at 350° for 10 to 15 minutes.

ARTICHOKE SQUARES

3 6-ounce jars marinated artichoke hearts
1 clove garlic
½ cup chopped onion
4 eggs
¼ cup seasoned bread crumbs
½ pound sharp Cheddar cheese, grated
2 Tablespoons minced parsley
¼ teaspoon salt
⅛ teaspoon each oregano, pepper, tabasco sauce

Drain oil from one jar of artichokes into 12-inch skillet and gently heat oil. Sauté onion and garlic in oil for five minutes and set aside. Drain and discard oil from the two remaining jars of artichokes, chop all the artichokes finely and set aside.

In medium bowl, beat eggs until foamy and blend in bread crumbs, cheese, parsley and remaining spices. Add chopped hearts and stir gently to blend. Add onion and garlic mixture and mix well. Spoon into greased 9x9-inch pan and bake at 325° for 30 minutes. Cool before cutting into 2-inch squares.

Can be baked ahead and reheated at 350° for 10 to 12 minutes just before serving.

Makes 16 servings.

LIPTAUER CHEESE

Mounded in a hollowed-out, rich brown pumpernickel loaf and surrounded by colorful garnishes, this rose-tinted, easy-to-do spread makes a spectacular presentation.

1 pound 3 ounces cream cheese, softened
6 ounces sharp Cheddar cheese, softened
5 Tablespoons unsalted butter, softened
1½ to 2 teaspoons Dijon mustard
2 Tablespoons chopped onion
Sweet Hungarian paprika
1 round loaf pumpernickle bread about
  14 to 16 inches in diameter

Garnishes

2 cans anchovy fillets, rinsed and chopped
⅔ cup finely chopped green onion
⅔ cup finely chopped green onion
⅔ cup diced radishes
½ cup drained capers
Small squares of pumpernickel, rye and black bread

Up to four days before serving (Liptauer must have time to mellow and should not be prepared less than one day before serving), combine cream cheese, Cheddar, butter, mustard and onion in food processor and blend until smooth. Add enough paprika to give a rosy color. (If using an electric mixer, chop cheddar into small dices and beat with other ingredients until smooth.) Refrigerate until morning of serving.

That morning, hollow out pumpernickel loaf by removing the top third and scooping out some of bread interior. (This bread can be reserved for crumbs.) Mound Liptauer in loaf, cover completely with plastic wrap and refrigerate.

Place garnishes in small bowls or crocks, cover with plastic and refrigerate.

Shortly before serving, set out filled loaf, garnishes and bread.

Serves 12.

DOUBLE CHEESE DELIGHT

6 to 8 ounces grated Swiss cheese
2 Tablespoons grated Parmesan cheese
3 green onions, finely chopped
Real mayonnaise
Paprika
Party rye or rye melba toast (halved)
  or crisp rye crackers

Mix two cheeses and onion. Add enough mayonnaise to make a good spreading consistency.

Pile generously on party rye or melba toast. (Do several hours before so flavor penetrates.) Place on cookie sheet and sprinkle with more Parmesan cheese and paprika. Place in 425° oven and watch for the cheese to bubble (4 to 6 minutes).

Serve immediately!

Serves 6 to 8.

CHEESE BALL

½ pound grated Cheddar cheese
8 ounces cream cheese
3 to 4 ounces Roquefort cheese
1 medium onion, minced
2 Tablespoons Worcestershire sauce
Chopped pecans

Combine all ingredients except pecans in mixer or food processor. Chill.

Form into 2 large or 5 small balls. Roll in chopped pecans.

Can be frozen. Thaw in refrigerator.

FESTIVE CHEESE BALL

1 pound cream cheese, softened
10 ounces shredded sharp Cheddar cheese
1 8½-ounce can crushed pineapple, drained
2 Tablespoons chopped green onion
2 teaspoons Worcestershire sauce
⅔ cup chopped walnuts

Thoroughly blend cream cheese and Cheddar cheese. Fold in pineapple, onion and Worcestershire sauce. Refrigerate several hours, shape into ball and roll in nuts. Refrigerate overnight.

Serve with crackers.

SALMON AND CREAM CHEESE SPREAD

12 ounces canned salmon, drained
6 ounces cream cheese, softened
2 Tablespoons light cream
¼ teaspoon onion salt
½ teaspoon dill weed

Thoroughly blend ingredients together.

Serve with crackers.

CARROT SPREAD

Best served on Ritz crackers.

5 to 6 large carrots, grated
8 ounces cream cheese, softened
1 Tablespoon grated onion
½ cup mayonnaise
1 Tablespoon Worcestershire sauce
Dash of Tabasco sauce

Combine ingredients and chill.

CHUTNEY CHEESE BALL

8 ounces cream cheese, softened
⅓ cup minced chutney
¼ cup sliced almonds
1 teaspoon curry powder
¼ teaspoon dry mustard
Coconut to coat (optional)

Mix all ingredients except coconut and shape into ball. Wrap in foil and chill until firm. Unwrap and roll in coconut. Rewrap in fresh foil and chill until ready to use.

CHEESE LOG

Fresh cream cheese makes this extra special.

½ pound Roquefort cheese
1 pound cream cheese
½ cup chopped celery
½ cup chopped green pepper
1 Tablespoon chopped onion
1 Tablespoon chopped parsley
1½ Tablespoons melted butter
Dash of salt
Chopped walnuts

Mix all ingredients except walnuts and shape into 1 large or 2 small logs.

Roll in chopped walnuts. Wrap in waxed paper and freeze for 24 hours before serving. Thaw in refrigerator.

WHITE SANGRIA

1 bottle (750 ml) dry white wine
½ cup Curacao
¼ cup granulated sugar
1 orange, thinly sliced
1 lemon, thinly sliced
1 lime, thinly sliced
4 or 5 large strawberries, sliced
1 10-ounce bottle club soda
Ice cubes

Combine wine, Curacao and sugar in pitcher and stir until sugar is dissolved. Add sliced fruits. Cover and chill in refrigerator at least 1 hour to let flavors blend.

Just before serving, add soda and ice cubes and stir gently to mix. Serve in wine glasses or Champagne flutes.

Makes 6
servings

LIME COOLER

2 cups cracked ice
1 6-ounce can frozen limeade concentrate, partially thawed
¼ cup lemon juice
1¼ cups vodka
1 10-ounce bottle club soda, chilled
Fresh strawberries, pineapple cubes and mint sprigs (garnish)

Combine ice, limeade concentrate and lemon juice in blender and mix at medium speed 1 minute. Add vodka and blend well. Pour in soda and mix briefly on low speed. Serve in stemmed goblets, and garnish as desired.

Makes 6 servings

FISHHOUSE PUNCH

2 fifths light rum
1 fifth brandy
Juice of one dozen lemons (3 cups)
Juice of ½ dozen oranges (2⅓ cups)
1 pound sugar (2 cups)
2 cups hot water
1 pint strong tea

Make syrup of sugar and water. Mix all ingredients. *Let stand a day.* Before serving, add:

2 quarts ginger ale
2 quarts soda

Makes two large punch bowls, full.

FRUIT FLOAT

3 cups chopped fruit (pineapple, oranges, peaches, apricots, strawberries)
1 bottle brandy or rum
1 cup sugar
3 bottles dry white wine
fresh fruit to garnish
soda (optional)

Soak fruit, sugar and brandy or rum overnight.

Place in a punch bowl with a large block of ice. Pour in white wine and garnish with fresh fruit.

Serve straight, or pour into glasses and top with soda to taste.

Serves 24-30

ORANGE VERMOUTH

1 bottle dry vermouth
½ bottle curacao
2½ cups orange juice
crushed ice
soda
cucumber peel

Mix vermouth, curacao and orange juice in jug with several handfuls of crushed ice.

Half fill 10-oz. glasses with orange mixture and fill with soda.

Serves 12-15

sauces and condiments

LEMON BUTTER

Serve over cooked asparagus or broccoli.

¼ cup butter or margarine
Grated rind and juice of ½ lemon
1 Tablespoon toasted sesame seeds
1 teaspoon sugar
¼ teaspoon garlic salt

Melt butter. Blend in remaining ingredients.

Makes
½ cup

HERB BUTTER

¼ cup butter
½ teaspoon salt
⅛ teaspoon pepper
2 teaspoons finely chopped parsley
1 teaspoon dried thyme or marjoram
1 teaspoon dried basil
1 glove garlic, crushed

Soften butter, add remaining ingredients and beat to blend well. Spread on French bread, cut diagonally without cutting all the way through. Wrap in aluminum foil. Heat in 400° oven for 10 minutes. Serve very hot.

D's PYRACANTHA JELLY

The pyracantha bush grows in and around the desert of Arizona and produces a juicy berry in the winter months.

1 quart pyracantha berries
5 cups water
1 cup *fresh* grapefruit juice
½ cup *fresh* lemon juice
1 1¾-ounce package powdered pectin
5½ cups sugar

Combine berries and water. Boil 30 minutes, mashing a few berries. Pour into cloth or colander and squeeze, reserving juice. Measure 3 cups berry juice. Add the grapefruit and lemon juices, combine with pectin in pan and bring to a boil. Add sugar and stir to dissolve. Bring to a rolling boil again for 2 minutes. Skim top. Pour into sterile glasses and seal.

Yield:
8 glasses

LEMON CURD

Use as jam on muffins or bread.

4 teaspoons grated lemon peel
⅔ cup lemon juice
5 eggs
1 cup sugar
½ cup melted butter

Put first four ingredients in blender and whirl til smooth. Gradually add butter. Transfer to saucepan and cook over medium heat until mixture begins to bubble and thicken. Pour into container.

Will keep in refrigerator 1 week. May be frozen.

Makes
2½ cups

DELICIOUS HAM SAUCE

½ cup raisins
2 cups sour cream
½ teaspoon salt
1 Tablespoon horseradish
2 Tablespoons lemon juice

Soften raisins in enough boiling water to cover, for 10 minutes. Drain.

Mix raisins with remaining ingredients. Store in refrigerator.

Serve at room temperature.

Makes
3 cups

SYBIL AMES' HOT ENGLISH MUSTARD

This makes a wonderful Christmas gift from your kitchen. A delicious spread for all meats and cheeses.

1 cup malt or cider vinegar
1 cup granulated sugar
1 cup dry mustard
3 whole eggs, beaten

Combine vinegar, sugar and mustard; whirl in blender and store overnight in the refrigerator.

Add beaten eggs and cook slowly in top of a double boiler, stirring frequently, until the consistency of boiled custard. Refrigerate. Keeps up to 1 year in the refrigerator. Does not freeze.

Makes
1 pint

MUSTARD SAUCE

Very good on meat.

1 Tablespoon butter
1 egg
¼ cup firmly packed brown sugar
3 Tablespoons granulated sugar
2 Tablespoons dry mustard
1 teaspoon paprika
⅓ cup cider vinegar

Melt butter in pan and cool.

Beat egg, sugars, mustard and paprika together. Beat in vinegar and cooled butter. Put in saucepan and stir over low heat 4 or 5 minutes until thickened. Cool.

Store in the refrigerator.

Makes
1½ cups.

PARTY PICKLES

- 1½ cups sugar
- 1 cup cider vinegar
- ¼ cup water
- ¼ teaspoon ground ginger
- 1 32-ounce jar kosher dills, sliced into quarters lengthwise
- 1 medium white onion, sliced in very thin rings
- 4 cinnamon sticks

Cook sugar, vinegar, water and ginger on medium heat until sugar is dissolved. Bring to a boil, simmer and cook until syrup is clear.

Place pickles and onions in alternate layers in large bowl. Pour syrup over. Add cinnamon sticks and cool. Cover and refrigerate for at least 2 days before serving.

CORN RELISH

2 cups chopped onions
2½ Tablespoons celery seed
1 Tablespoon mustard seed
2 cups vinegar
2 Tablespoons salt
2 cups granulated sugar
2 quarts whole canned corn, drained
1 cup pickle relish
1½ cups chopped pimiento or red bell pepper
2 cups diced celery

Combine first six ingredients and boil 5 minutes; then cool. Combine remaining ingredients into cooked mixture; chill and serve.

Makes 3 quarts

ZUCCHINI SQUASH RELISH

10 cups chopped zucchini
4 cups chopped onions
2½ cups apple cider vinegar
4½ cups sugar
2½ teaspoons celery salt
1½ teaspoons pepper
1 teaspoon nutmeg
½ teaspoon tumeric
4 Tablespoons cornstarch
1 chopped red pepper

Sprinkle salt over chopped zucchini. Let stand for several hours.

Drain; rinse; drain again. Combine remaining ingredients in large pan and add zucchini. Bring to a boil, stirring constantly. Pour in jars when consistency of relish. Seal.

Makes 6 pints.

APPLE CHUTNEY

6 ripe tomatoes
3 pounds apples
2 pounds onions
2 pounds white sugar
¼ cup salt
1 quart vinegar
1 teaspoon cayenne pepper
1 Tablespoon cinnamon

Quarter tomatoes, apples and onions and put through grinder or food processor. Transfer to large cooking pan, add remaining ingredients, bring to a boil and simmer, uncovered, for one hour.

Pour in glass jars and seal with lids.

HOT CURRIED FRUIT

1 16-ounce can sliced pineapple
1 29-ounce can pear halves
1 29-ounce can peach halves
⅓ cup butter
½ cup brown sugar
1½ teaspoons curry powder
⅛ teaspoon salt
Juice of ½ lemon

Drain fruit thoroughly, reserving ¼ cup juice, and pat dry with a towel. Arrange fruit in shallow baking dish.

Melt butter and stir in reserved fruit juice, brown sugar, curry powder, salt and lemon juice. Dribble over fruit. Let stand in refrigerator, covered, overnight.

Bake, uncovered, 45 minutes at 375°. Freezes well.

HOT SHERRIED FRUIT CASSEROLE

Excellent with chicken or ham. Delightful topping over ice cream.

1 16-ounce can sliced pineapple
1 16-ounce can peach halves
1 16-ounce can pear halves
1 16-ounce can apricot halves
1 14-ounce jar apple rings

Sauce
½ cup butter
2 heaping Tablespoons flour
½ cup light brown sugar
1 cup sherry

Drain fruit and arrange in layers in a 2-quart casserole, with apple rings on top.

Prepare sauce by cooking in double boiler until thick and smooth. Pour hot sauce over fruit. Cover and refrigerate overnight or several days.

Bake uncovered at 350° until hot and bubbly, about 30 minutes.

Makes 2 quarts

ORANGE PEEL CREAM CHEESE

The plentiful citrus crop in Arizona makes this a local favorite.

½ cup cream cheese, softened
3 Tablespoons unsalted butter, softened
2 Tablespoons fresh orange juice
1 Tablespoon honey
1 Tablespoon grated orange peel
1 teaspoon fresh lemon juice

Combine all ingredients in blender and mix until just blended. Taste and adjust flavor, adding more honey if sweeter spread is desired.

Cover and refrigerate until ready to serve.

Serve with carrot cake or sweet bread.

Makes 1 cup

salads and dressings

TACO SALAD

Guests enjoy "building their own."

1 pound ground beef
1 large onion, chopped
1 16-ounce can pinto or kidney beans
Taco sauce to taste
1 package dry taco seasoning
8 ounces corn chips
8 ounces thousand island dressing
1 head lettuce, shredded
4 tomatoes, diced
1 avocado, diced
½ pound Cheddar cheese, grated
Sour cream

Brown ground beef and onion, drain and put in bowl. Add beans, taco sauce, taco seasoning, ¼ of corn chips, crushed, and the salad dressing. Toss to mix.

In another bowl combine lettuce, tomatoes, avocado and cheese.

In separate bowls, set out chips and sour cream.

Build salad as follows: Place a few chips on plate, add lettuce mixture, hot mixture, lettuce, more hot mixture, dollop of sour cream and top with chips.

Serves 6

CORNED BEEF SALAD

1 12-ounce can corned beef
1 10-ounce can beef bouillon
1 3-ounce package lemon jello
3 hard-boiled eggs, chopped
1 small onion, grated
2 teaspoons finely diced green pepper
1 cup diced celery
1 cup mayonnaise

Heat bouillon and pour over jello. Stir until dissolved. Cool until slightly thickened.

Add vegetables, eggs, and meat which has been broken up with a fork.

Stir in mayonnaise.

Pour into 8 x 11-inch pan and chill until set.

Serves 10.

EMPEROR'S CHICKEN AND SHRIMP SALAD

4 cups uncooked elbow macaroni
2 14-ounce cans sweetened condensed milk
2 cups lemon juice
2 cups vegetable oil
½ cup prepared mustard
6 cups diced cooked chicken
2 cups shelled and deveined cooked shrimp
1 20-ounce can pineapple chunks, drained
1 16-ounce can peaches, diced and drained
1 cup minced celery
½ cup chopped green onion
Orange slices and sieved hardboiled eggs
for garnish - optional

Cook macaroni as package directs; rinse and drain.

In 8-quart bowl, combine sweetened condensed milk, lemon juice, vegetable oil, and mustard, blending until smooth. Fold in macaroni, chicken, shrimp, pineapple, peaches, celery, and onion. Chill several hours to blend flavors.

Serve on lettuce leaves garnished with orange slices and sieved hard boiled eggs.

Can be prepared up to 36 hours ahead of time.

Serves 16 to 20

LAYERED SPINACH SALAD

2 cups torn spinach pieces
8 slices bacon, diced and fried
6 hard-cooked eggs, sliced
2 cups iceberg lettuce
8 ounces water chestnuts, sliced
10 ounces frozen peas, thawed
½ cup chopped Bermuda onion
1 cup mayonnaise
1 cup Miracle Whip
1 cup shredded Monterey Jack cheese

Layer first seven ingredients, in order given, in 9″ x 13″ dish. Combine mayonnaise and Miracle Whip and spread dressing over salad, sealing well. Sprinkle with cheese and cover tightly with plastic wrap.

Refrigerate at least 24 hours.

Keeps well for 48 additional hours.

Serves 6.

CHICKEN SALAD WITH CURRY

3 cups cooked and diced chicken
1 cup chopped celery
½ teaspoon salt
2 teaspoons lemon juice
1 cup mayonnaise
2 teaspoons soy sauce
2 teaspoons curry powder
1 cup seedless grapes or diced pineapple
1 can mandarin oranges, drained
¾ cup sliced almonds or pecans, toasted

Combine chicken, celery, salt and lemon juice.

Mix mayonnaise, soy sauce and curry powder together. Mix well with chicken. Add fruits and mix well. Chill.

Mix nuts into salad just before serving.

Serves 10.

SHRIMP CHOW MEIN SALAD

2 10-oz. packages frozen peas,
thawed but not cooked
6 ounces frozen baby shrimp
1 cup chopped celery
1 onion, minced
¾ cup mayonnaise
1 teaspoon lemon juice
⅛ teaspoon curry
1 teaspoon soy sauce
½ teaspoon garlic salt
2½ ounces slivered almonds, or
¾ cup sunflower seeds
1 5-ounce can chow mein noodles

Toss first nine ingredients until thoroughly mixed. Chill to blend flavors.

Just before serving fold in nuts or seeds and noodles.

SEAFOOD LOUIS MOLD

3 envelopes unflavored gelatin
1 cup water
1 10¾-ounce can condensed tomato soup
1 cup sour cream
1 cup mayonnaise
2 teaspoons Worcestershire sauce
5 drops Tabasco sauce
⅓ cup catsup
1 cup chopped celery
½ cup thinly sliced green onions
3 Tablespoons sweet pickle relish
½ pound small shrimp, peeled and deveined, cooked
½ pound flaked crab meat

Sprinkle gelatin over water in a small bowl.

Bring soup to a boil in small sauce pan over moderate heat, making sure soup is very hot. Stir in gelatin, remove from heat and stir until gelatin is completely dissolved.

In large bowl, mix sour cream, mayonnaise and soup mixture until smooth. Stir in Worcestershire, tabasco and catsup. Refrigerate about 30 minutes.

Fold in vegetables, relish, shrimp and crabmeat.

Rinse a 6 cup mold with cold water. Fill with mixture, cover and refrigerate 4 hours or longer, until firm. Unmold and serve.

BAKED SEAFOOD SALAD

1 cup sliced fresh mushrooms
4 Tablespoons butter
1 6-ounce can crab meat, drained
2 4½-ounce cans shrimp, drained and rinsed
1 green pepper, diced
2 cups diced celery
2 cups mayonnaise
4 hard-boiled eggs, chopped
1 Tablespoon lemon juice
1 teaspoon salt
2 teaspoon Worcestershire sauce
1 5-ounce can water chestnuts, drained and sliced
½ cup bread crumbs, buttered

Sauté mushrooms in butter. Toss together with next ten ingredients. Place in 8″ x 12″ pyrex dish. Cover with bread crumbs and bake at 350° for 30 minutes.

Serves 8.

HOT CRABMEAT-AVOCADO SALAD

1 7½-ounce can crabmeat, drained
⅓ cup chopped celery
3 hard boiled eggs, chopped
2 Tablespoons chopped pimiento
1 Tablespoon chopped onion
½ teaspoon salt
½ cup mayonnaise
4 ripe avocados
lemon juice
salt
3 Tablespoons dry bread crumbs
1 teaspoon melted butter
2 Tablespoons slivered almonds

Mix crabmeat, celery, eggs, pimiento, onion, salt and mayonniase.

Cut unpeeled avocados in half lengthwise; remove pits. Brush halves with lemon juice, sprinkle lightly with salt.

Fill avocado halves with crabmeat mixture.

Toss bread crumbs in butter; spoon over crabmeat. Place in greased shallow baking dish; bake uncovered 10 minutes at 400°.

Sprinkle almonds over crumb topping; bake 5 minutes longer or until bubbly.

Serves 6 to 8

SPAGHETTI SALAD

6 cups cooked spaghetti, well drained
1½ Tablespoons oil
2 cups finely shredded red cabbage
1½ cups finely chopped green onion
12 radishes, finely sliced
1 medium cucumber, finely sliced
and cut in quarters
1 cup finely chopped celery
Salt and pepper to taste
Soy sauce dressing (see below)
Bean sprouts
2 Hard boiled eggs, sliced

Soy Sauce Dressing
1 cup mayonnaise
1 Tablespoon soy sauce
2 Tablespoons grated onion

Cut the cooked spaghetti 2 or 3 times; toss with oil and chill for 2 hours. Mix spaghetti with cabbage, onions, radishes, cucumbers, celery and soy sauce dressing. Salt and pepper to taste. Garnish with bean sprouts and egg slices.

PASTA-VEGETABLE SALAD

Fresh vegetables are a must for this salad.

- 12 ounces vermicelli spaghetti
- 2 cups fresh broccoli flowerettes
- 6 to 8 ounces fresh pea pods
- 1 large carrot, shredded
- ½ package Italian dressing mix
- ⅓ teaspoon garlic salt
- ⅔ cup grated Parmesan & Romano cheese
- ¾ cup Italian dressing

Cook spaghetti and drain. Rinse with cold water.

Cook broccoli, pea pods and carrots — separately — briefly, just until tender-crisp. Rinse in cold water immediately. Combine all together in bowl with remaining ingredients. Refrigerate. Chill thoroughly, toss and serve.

Serves
6 to 8

SUPER COLE SLAW

1 teaspoon salt
½ teaspoon pepper
½ teaspoon dry mustard
1 teaspoon celery seed
2 Tablespoons sugar
3 Tablespoons oil
⅓ cup vinegar
1 teaspoon grated onion
⅓ cup chopped green pepper
4 cups chopped cabbage

In medium sized bowl, place salt, pepper, dry mustard, celery seed, sugar, oil, and vinegar. Mix thoroughly. Add onion, green pepper, and cabbage, tossing to coat well. Seal bowl and refrigerate.

This salad is best if made 24 hours ahead of serving time and will keep up to 1 week, refrigerated.

Serves 8.

CAULIFLOWER COLESLAW

Great with barbecue!

1 medium head cauliflower, very thinly sliced
1 cup thinly sliced radishes
1 small onion, grated
½ cup snipped watercress
¾ teaspoon salt
Dash of pepper

Dressing
1 cup sour cream
½ package garlic cheese salad dressing mix
¼ teaspoon seasoned salt
1½ Tablespoon lemon juice
2 Tablespoons salad oil

Prepare dressing ahead of time and refrigerate.

Mix vegetables with salt and pepper. Add dressing and mix well.

Serves 6

MARINATED ZUCCHINI

1 pound small zucchini, thinly sliced
1 10-ounce package frozen green peas with pearl onions
½ cup Italian dressing
2 Tablespoons wine vinegar
Salad Greens

Cover zucchini with boiling salted water. Let stand one minute and drain.

Cook peas as directed and drain.

Combine vegetables with salad dressing and vinegar. Cover and chill.

Line a chilled bowl with salad greens. Stir vegetables gently and spoon into bowl.

Serves 6

GRANDMA BONE'S VEGETABLE SALAD

This is a dieter's delight!!!

Lettuce
Bermuda onion, sliced
Cucumber, finely sliced
Carrots, finely sliced
Lettuce
Radishes, finely sliced
Tomato, sliced
Juice from one lemon

Layer the vegetables in order given in a large salad bowl, with coarse ground salt and ground pepper on each layer. Cover and chill for at least 3 hours.

Squeeze juice from one lemon over salad just before serving.

KOREAN SPINACH SALAD

The dressing makes this salad something special!

1 pound spinach, torn in pieces
3 hard boiled eggs, diced
6 to 8 slices bacon, fried and crumbled
2 cups bean sprouts
1 8-ounce can water chestnuts, drained

Dressing
1 cup olive oil
⅔ cup sugar
Salt to taste
1 medium onion, grated
¼ cup vinegar
⅓ cup catsup
1 Tablespoon Worcestershire sauce

For dressing, blend all ingredients in food processor and chill until serving time.

Combine salad ingredients and toss with dressing just before serving.

Serves 4 to 6

MANDARIN TOSSED SALAD

½ cup sliced almonds
2 Tablespoons sugar
2 teaspoons water
1 head lettuce (red leaf or romaine)
6 green onions, sliced
1 4-ounce can mandarin oranges, drained

Dressing
⅓ cup salad oil
3 Tablespoons sugar
3 Tablespoons vinegar
1 teaspoon salt
1 dash pepper

Combine almonds, sugar and water in shallow glass baking dish.

Microwave 2½ to 3½ minutes, stirring occasionally or bake 15 to 20 minutes at 400°, stirring occasionally.

Combine lettuce and green onion; combine dressing ingredients.

Add dressing to salad greens and toss. Top with oranges and glazed almonds.

Serves 6

CITRUS SALAD

4 large oranges
2 avocados
2 to 4 Tablespoons honey, according to taste
4 Tablespoons tarragon wine vinegar
Salt
Lemon or lime juice
4 Tablespoon capers

Chill oranges and avocados.

Blend honey and tarragon vinegar.

Peel oranges and cut into bite-sized chunks. Peel avocados, cut into bite-sized chunks and sprinkle with salt and lemon juice. Combine orange and avocado chunks.

Place on crisp lettuce.

Pour honey-vinegar dressing over. Garnish with capers.

Serves 4

CRANBERRY SALAD MOLD

1 3½-ounce package cherry gelatin
½ cup sugar
1½ cups boiling water
1 cup raw cranberries, chopped
¼ cup ground orange, rind included
1 banana, thinly sliced
¾ cup black walnuts, broken
8-ounce can crushed pineapple, well drained

Dissolve gelatin and sugar in water. Let cool and stir in remaining ingredients.

Pour into jello mold and chill until set.

Serves 4 to 6

APPLEBERRY SALAD

1 3-ounce package raspberry or strawberry gelatin
1 cup boiling water
1 10-ounce box frozen raspberries or strawberries, slightly thawed, not drained
1½ cups applesauce
Sour cream or whipped cream

Dissolve gelatin in water. Add berries and juice; stir until well thawed. Add applesauce and mix well. Pour into 4 cup mold and chill until firm. Serve with topping.

Makes
4 cups

WEDDING RING MOLDED SALAD

1 3-ounce package lime gelatin
¾ cup boiling water
¾ cup milk
1 cup cottage cheese
1 cup crushed pineapple, drained slightly
1 cup shredded cabbage

Dissolve gelatin in water; cool to room temperature and add milk. Pour over cabbage, cottage cheese and pineapple, mixing well. Pour into an oiled, 6-cup ring mold and chill until serving time.

Serves
6 to 8

HOLIDAY JELLIED SALAD

1 6-ounce package orange gelatin
1 3-ounce package strawberry gelatin
2 cups boiling water
2 13-ounce cans crushed pineapple
Orange juice
1 16-ounce can whole cranberry sauce
1 11-ounce can mandarin oranges
2 apples, chopped
1 cup chopped nuts

Dissolve gelatin in boiling water.

Drain pineapple, reserving juice; add orange juice to equal 2 cups and add the 2 cups of juice to the gelatin. Chill until partially set.

Add fruit and nuts, pour into a two quart mold and chill until fully set.

Unmold on a bed of salad greens.

Serves 16

UNDER-THE-SEA SALAD

1 pound can pear halves
¾ cup pear syrup
1 3-ounce package lime gelatin
¼ teaspoon salt
1 cup boiling water
1 Tablespoon lemon juice
6 ounces cream cheese, softened
⅛ teaspoon ginger

Drain pears, reserving ¾ cup pear syrup; add water to fill, if necessary.

Dissolve gelatin and salt in boiling water. Add pear syrup and lemon juice and measure 1¼ cups into a one quart mold. Chill until set, but not firm.

Meanwhile, beat cheese until creamy. Gradually add remaining gelatin, blending until smooth. Add the ginger and chill until very thick.

Dice pears and fold into cheese mixture. Spoon into mold. Chill until firm. Unmold on crisp lettuce.

Serves 8

PINK ARCTIC FREEZE

For luncheon, serve with dainty sandwiches — or pass cookies and let it be a dessert!

- 6 ounces cream cheese, softened
- 2 Tablespoons mayonnaise or salad dressing
- 2 Tablespoons granulated sugar
- 1 pound can whole cranberry sauce
- 1 9-ounce can crushed pineapple or pineapple tidbits, drained
- ½ cup chopped walnuts
- 1 cup whipping cream, whipped

Blend cream cheese, mayonnaise and sugar. Add fruits and nuts. Fold in whipped cream. Pour into a loaf pan. Freeze firm, 6 hours or overnight.

To serve, let stand at room temperature about 15 minutes, turn out and slice.

Serves
8 to 10

CILE'S FROZEN FRUIT SALAD

- 1 pint sour cream
- ½ cup sugar
- 2 Tablespoons lemon juice
- 1 8-ounce can pineapple tidbits or crushed pineapple
- 2 bananas, cut up
- ½ cup chopped pecans
- 5 ounces maraschino cherries

Combine all ingredients. Spoon into fluted paper cups in muffin tins. Cover with foil and freeze. Or, pour into freezer tray, cover and freeze.

About 10 minutes before serving time, remove from freezer and place on lettuce.

Serves
10 to 12

TOMATO ASPIC

Not the typical aspic.

1 3-ounce package lemon gelatin
1 cup boiling water
1 cup tomato sauce
1 3-ounce jar stuffed olives, sliced
1 4½-ounce can shrimp, drained
1 cup chopped celery
3 hard boiled eggs, chopped
4 green onions, chopped
1 teaspoon Worcestershire sauce
3 Tablespoons lemon juice

Dissolve gelatin in water. Add remaining ingredients and pour into a one quart mold (oiled with mayonnaise) and chill until serving time.

Serves 4 to 6

RUBY SALAD DRESSING

1 cup salad oil
1 cup sugar
⅔ cup catsup
½ cup vinegar
½ teaspoon paprika
1 teaspoon salt
2 Tablespoons grated onion

Mix oil and sugar well and refrigerate overnight.

Add remaining ingredients to oil and sugar and beat 15 minutes in mixer at medium speed or in blender for 10 minutes. Refrigerate 24 hours before serving.

Keeps in refrigerator for several weeks.

Makes
3 cups.

FRANNIE'S GARLIC DRESSING

This dressing improves with age.

1½ cups vegetable oil
¼ cup cider vinegar
¼ garlic wine vinegar
4 garlic cloves, halved
¼ teaspoon dry mustard
1 teaspoon salt
1 teaspoon garlic salt
1 teaspoon ground pepper

Combine all ingredients in jar; shake well and chill.

Makes
2 cups

GARLIC SALAD DRESSING

Wonderful on green salad.

⅔ cup salad oil
⅓ cup vinegar
¼ teaspoon paprika
1 teaspoon salt
1 Tablespoon sugar
2 garlic cloves, split
1 bay leaf

Mix all ingredients together. Let stand overnight *before* chilling.

Makes
1 cup

soups and bread

BROCCOLI-CAULIFLOWER SOUP

1 8-ounce package frozen cauliflower
1 10¾-ounce can condensed chicken broth
1 10-ounce package frozen chopped broccoli
½ teaspoon mustard seed
½ teaspoon dried dillweed
½ teaspoon ground mace
⅓ cup finely chopped onion
¼ cup butter or margarine
2 Tablespoons all-purpose flour
½ teaspoon salt
3½ cups milk
1 cup shredded process Swiss cheese (4 ounces)

In a 3-quart saucepan cook cauliflower, covered, in *half* of the chicken broth for 5 to 8 minutes or until tender. In a medium saucepan combine remaining chicken broth, broccoli, mustard seed and dillweed. Cook, covered, for 5 to 8 minutes or until broccoli is tender. Set aside a few broccoli heads for garnish, if desired. Remove from heat, cover and keep warm. Place cauliflower mixture and mace in blender or food processor and blend until smooth. In the 3-quart saucepan, cook onion in butter until almost tender. Stir in flour, salt and pepper. Add milk all at once, cook and stir until thickened and bubbly. Stir sauce, cauliflower mixture and cheese into broccoli mixture, cook and stir until heated through and cheese is melted. Garnish with reserved broccoli.

Serves 4 to 6

CREAMY POTATO SOUP

Follow exactly — perfect everytime!

8 to 10 slices bacon
1 cup chopped onion
4 to 5 cups cubed raw potatoes
2 cups water
2 10½-ounce cans cream of chicken soup
2 cans milk
1 teaspoon salt
2 packages smokie links, sliced

Fry bacon in deep soup pan and remove. Pour off all but 3 Tablespoons drippings and sauté onion. Add potatoes, water and sausage slices. Cook covered 15 minutes or until potatoes are tender. Drain. Blend in remaining ingredients. Crumble bacon and add. Heat but do not boil.

Serves 6 to 8

WHITE BEAN SOUP

2 celery stalks, sliced
1 medium onion, sliced
1 medium leek (or another onion), sliced
3 Tablespoons butter
6 cups chicken stock
1½ cups canned white beans, rinsed
1 bay leaf
2 teaspoons salt
1 or *more* garlic cloves
Milk or cream to thin

In a heavy saucepan sauté celery, onions and leek in butter until limp. Add stock and bring to a boil. Add beans, bay leaf and salt and return to boil and immediately remove from heat. Let sit until the beans are heated through, stirring occasionally. Puree the soup. Squeeze garlic, adding just the juice and return soup to pan to reheat before serving. Thin with milk or cream so the texture is pleasant.

Yield 2 quarts

BROCCOLI-POTATO SOUP

1½ cups minced leeks
¼ cup minced onion
1 large clove garlic, minced
3 Tablespoons minced carrot
4 Tablespoons butter
4 cups chicken stock
1½ cups diced potatoes
1½ cups cooked chopped broccoli
1½ Tablespoons grated onion
1 cup half and half
Salt and pepper to taste

Sauté leeks, onion, garlic and carrot in butter until leeks are soft. Do not brown. Add stock and potatoes; cover, bring to a boil and simmer until potatoes are tender. Add broccoli and onion and simmer 10 minutes. Puree in blender. Add cream, reheat, then salt and pepper to taste.

Serves 6

FLEMISH SOUP

Equally good using broccoli or cauliflower.

18 ounces frozen brussel sprouts
3 medium onions, quartered
6 medium potatoes, peeled and quartered
1 10¾-ounce can chicken broth
3 cups cream, half and half or milk
2 ounces unsalted butter
Salt and white pepper to taste

Cover brussel sprouts, onions and potatoes with chicken broth. Simmer gently until tender. Blend until smooth. Add cream, salt and pepper and unsalted butter. Heat on medium until hot.

This soup can be frozen *after* it has been blended. Thaw and add cream, salt, pepper and unsalted butter.

Serve with a dash of paprika and a sprig of parsley.

SOUPE A L'OIGNON

6 large Spanish onions, peeled and sliced
½ cup olive oil
3 cups Chablis
Thyme
1 bay leaf
8 cups boiling water
8 teaspoons beef seasoned stock base
Salt and pepper to taste
8 slices 2″ round French bread
1 pound Swiss cheese

Saute onions in very hot oil until brown. Add Chablis, thyme, bay leaf, water and base. Simmer slowly for 30 minutes and season to taste. Pour into individual crocks, topping each with slice of bread and 2 ounces cheese. Broil until cheese is melted and browned; serve immediately.

Makes 8
servings

VICHYSSOISE

8 Tablespoons butter
3 cups sliced leeks or onions
½ cup chopped celery
8 cups fresh chicken stock
4 cups sliced potatoes
Salt and white pepper to taste
2 cups heavy cream
4 Tablespoons finely chopped chives

Melt butter and add leeks and celery. Cook 20 minutes until clear. Add stock, potatoes and seasonings. Simmer until potatoes are tender. Puree and chill. Stir in cream and garnish with chives just before serving.

CLAM CHOWDER

1 cup butter
4 cups diced onion
2 cups diced celery
2 cups diced carrots
6 cups diced potatoes
3 Tablespoons parsley
3 teaspoons salt
Freshly ground pepper to taste
½ teaspoon thyme
1 bay leaf
6 cups water
4 7½-ounce cans minced clams
1 to 1¼ cups cream

All vegetables should be diced into ¼-inch pieces. Melt butter in heavy stock pot. Sauté four vegetables with butter until tender. Add minced parsley, salt, thyme and pepper. Sauteing process should take 10 to 15 minutes over medium heat. Add water. Cook 30 to 40 minutes. Cool mixture slightly, remove 5 cups of mixture and puree in a blender or food processor. Pour puree mixture back. Add minced clams and juice. Allow chowder heating time and then add cream and continue heating until heated through.

Serves 12 to 15

MICROWAVE CLAM CHOWDER

Quick and very good.

2 slices bacon, diced
1 medium onion, diced
2 medium potatoes, diced
¼ cup chopped celery
2 or 3 7½-ounce cans minced clams
Reserved clam liquid plus water to equal 1 cup
2 cups milk
¼ cup butter, melted
¼ cup unsifted flour
¾ teaspoon salt
⅛ teaspoon pepper
Bay leaf

Place bacon in 3-quart casserole. Microwave on High for 3 minutes. Add onions, potatoes, celery and cover. Microwave on High for 5 minutes. Add clams and juice, cover and cook on High for 8 to 10 minutes, or until potatoes are tender. Melt butter and stir in flour. Add to mixture along with milk, salt, pepper and bay leaf. Cover and microwave on High for 5 minutes or until hot.

MARITATA SOUP

½ cup butter
¾ cup grated Jack cheese
¼ cup grated Romano or Parmesan cheese
4 egg yolks, well beaten
1 cup whipping cream
2 10¾-ounce cans condensed chicken broth
2 cans water
1 cup dry white wine
4 ounces coil vermicelli

Whip butter until soft. Blend in cheeses and egg yolks. Gradually mix in cream. Heat chicken broth and water. Add wine and vermicelli. Simmer 8 minutes. Mix a little hot broth into cheese mixture, stirring constantly — then stir into hot broth. Heat through but don't allow to boil. Sprinkle with minced parsley and grated Parmesan to serve.

Serves 4 to 6

GOULASH SOUP

This recipe comes from a little Inn in Hohenschwangan, Bavaria.

- 3 Tablespoons butter
- 1 pound pork, cut in ½ inch cubes
- 1 pound beef, cut in ½ inch cubes
- 3 cups chopped onions
- 2 Tablespoons paprika
- 1½ cups diced green peppers
- 1 cup canned tomatoes, drained and cut coarsley
- 6 cups boiling water
- 2 teaspoons salt
- ½ teaspoon freshly ground black pepper
- 2 cups cubed potatoes
- ½ pound smoked sausage, sliced

Brown pork, beef and onions in the butter in a saucepan. Sprinkle with paprika, stirring constantly. Add green pepper, tomatoes, water, salt and pepper. Bring to a boil. Cover and simmer for 1½ hours.

While soup is cooking, cover sausages with water, bring to a boil and cook 5 minutes. Drain, slice and add to soup. Adjust seasonings if necessary. At the end of the 1½ hour simmering period, add potatoes, and cook 20 minutes.

Serves 6 to 8

DICKY'S SOUP

1 pound ground chuck
¼ teaspoon pepper
1 teaspoon Worcestershire sauce
½ Tablespoon sugar
1 Tablespoon basil
1 16-ounce can tomatoes
1 8-ounce can tomato sauce
1½ cups cubed potatoes
½ cup chopped onion
1 cup chopped celery
½ cup chopped parsley
2 16-ounce cans beef bouillon
1 10-ounce package frozen mixed vegetables

Brown meat in heavy, deep saucepan. Add rest of ingredients except frozen vegetables. Simmer one hour. Add frozen vegetables and cook another hour.

Yields 2½ quarts

TACO SOUP

Spicy and hearty.

2½ pounds ground beef
2 7-ounce cans mild chile salsa
3 7-ounce cans taco sauce
1 4-ounce can diced green chiles
1 or 2 8-ounce cans tomato sauce
Garlic salt to taste

Brown ground beef with garlic salt in soup pot. Add chile salsa, taco sauce, green chiles and 1 or 2 cans tomato sauce, depending on consistency. It should be thick (like chili). Simmer 10 minutes. Serve in bowls with corn chips, chopped onion, grated longhorn cheese and shredded lettuce for garnish.

Serves 5

SWEDISH BAKED FRUIT SOUP

Delicious with meat, for brunches, dessert, on ice cream — a real variety dish.

- 1 16-ounce can whole cranberry sauce
- 1 20-ounce can pineapple slices
- 2 large apples, peeled and cut up
- 2 large oranges, peeled and sectioned
- ½ cup raisins
- ½ cup pineapple juice
- 2 Tablespoons cornstarch
- ¼ cup molasses
- ¼ cup melted butter

Break up cranberry sauce gently with fork. Drain pineapple, reserving ½ cup juice, and cut in pieces. Add apples, oranges and raisins. Put in 3-quart baking dish.

Mix juice and cornstarch until smooth. Add molasses and butter and mix. Pour over fruit mixture. Bake at 325° for 20-25 minutes.

Makes 10 to 12 servings.

COLD MELON SOUP

Good for summer brunch.

½ cup cantaloupe, in pieces
½ cup honeydew, in pieces
½ cup crenshaw melon, in pieces
2 cups orange juice
½ cup lime juice
2 Tablespoons honey
2 cups dry champagne

Reserve several pieces of fruit.

In blender or food processor, mix all ingredients, except champagne. Put in glass or ceramic bowl and add champagne. Cover and chill for 2 hours.

Garnish with reserved fruit, a dollop of whipped cream and mint leaves.

Serves 6.

WHITE GAZPACHO

Cool, wonderful summer soup.

3 medium cucumbers, peeled, seeded and cut into chunks
2 cups chicken broth
3 cups sour cream
3 Tablespoons white vinegar
2 teaspoons salt
1 clove garlic, crushed

Whirl cucumbers and 1 cup of chicken broth in blender or food processor a very short time (until finely chopped, not pureed). Combine with rest of chicken broth, vinegar, salt and garlic. Blend mixture gradually into sour cream. Chill well.

Serve in chilled bowls or mugs garnished with:

¾ cups chopped toasted almonds
2 tomatoes, seeded and chopped
½ cup sliced green onions
½ cup chopped fresh parsley

Serves 6 to 8

HONEY WHEAT BREAD

4 cups all-purpose flour
2 cups whole wheat flour
½ cup wheat germ
2½ cups warm water (110-115° F)
⅓ cup all-vegetable shortening
⅓ cup instant nonfat dry milk
2 packages active dry yeast
¼ cup honey
1 Tablespoon salt

Measure all-purpose flour, whole wheat flour and wheat germ into bowl; stir to mix. Set aside. Combine warm water, shortening, dry milk, yeast, honey, salt and 3 cups of flour mixture in large mixing bowl. Mix well on low speed, scraping sides and bottom of bowl often. Beat 3 minutes at medium speed. Gradually stir in remaining flour by hand to make stiff dough. Cover and let rest for 15 minutes.

Knead dough on floured surface until smooth, 1 or 2 minutes. Divide dough in half. Roll each half into a 12x6-inch rectangle. Starting at 6-inch side, roll up and place seam side down in greased 9x5x3-inch loaf pans. Cover and let rise in warm place until doubled, about 1 to 1½ hours. Bake in preheated 400° oven for 30 to 35 minutes. Remove from pan immediately and cool on wire racks.

Yield — 2 loaves.

CRUSTY BRAN BREAD

1 cup whole wheat flour
1 cup white flour
2 cups bran cereal
1 teaspoon soda
1½ teaspoon baking powder
1 teaspoon salt
6 Tablespoons brown sugar
3 Tablespoons shortening
1 cup buttermilk

Put all dry ingredients into large bowl. Add shortening to dry ingredients and blend until it is in fine pieces. Pour in buttermilk and mix well. Work dough with hands until it forms a rough ball. Shape into a round ball and place in greased 9-inch layer cake pan. Make partial cuts crosswise through dough. Brush surface with 1 Tablespoon melted butter. Crush ¼ cup bran with 2 Tablespoons sugar in blender. Sprinkle over top of loaf.

Bake in preheated 350° over for 35 to 40 minutes.

Yield — 1 loaf.

QUICK WHOLE WHEAT RAISIN-NUT BREAD

Makes exceptionally delicious toast.

- 3 cups whole wheat flour
- ¼ cup toasted wheat germ
- 2 teaspoons baking powder
- 1¼ teaspoons soda
- 1 teaspoon salt
- 1½ cups buttermilk
- ½ cup honey
- ¼ cup salad oil
- ½ cup raisins
- ½ cup chopped walnuts

Stir together flour, wheat germ, baking powder, soda and salt. Combine buttermilk, honey and oil and pour all at once into the flour mixture, stirring just until all ingredients are combined. Add raisins and nuts, being careful not to overmix the batter. Pour into greased 9½x5¼-inch loaf pan, and bake in a 325° oven for 1 hour and 15 minutes. Cool in pan for 10 minutes.

Yield — 1 loaf.

WHEAT GERM ZUCCHINI BREAD

3 eggs
1 cup oil
1 cup sugar
1 cup firmly packed brown sugar
3 teaspoons maple flavoring
2 cups coarsely shredded zucchini
2½ cups unsifted flour
½ cup toasted wheat germ
2 teaspoons soda
1 teaspoon salt
½ teaspoon baking powder
1 cup finely chopped walnuts
⅓ cup sesame seeds, optional

Preheat oven to 350°. Beat eggs well; add oil, sugars and maple flavoring. Stir in zucchini. Combine flour, wheat germ, soda, salt, baking powder and walnuts. Add to zucchini mixture. Divide batter between two 9x5x3-inch greased and floured loaf pans. Sprinkle with sesame seeds. Bake for 1 hour. Cool 10 minutes and remove from pan.

Yield — 2 loaves

PEACH PECAN BREAD

1 16-ounce can sliced peaches
6 Tablespoons butter or margarine, melted
2 eggs
1 Tablespoon lemon juice
2 cups flour
3 teaspoons baking powder
1 teaspoon salt
¾ cup chopped pecans
2 Tablespoons peach preserves

Drain peaches, reserving ¼ cup syrup. Finely chop 1 cup peaches, and set aside. In blender, combine remaining peaches, butter, eggs, peach syrup and lemon juice. Blend until smooth. Stir together dry ingredients, add egg mixture and stir until moistened. Fold in chopped peaches, pecans and preserves. Turn into a greased 8x4x2-inch loaf pan. Bake in 350° oven for 1 hour.

Yield — 1 loaf.

FRESH APPLE BREAD

2 cups flour
2 teaspoons baking powder
1 teaspoon salt
½ teaspoon cinnamon
¼ teaspoon grated nutmeg
½ cup butter, softened
1¼ cups sugar
2 eggs
2 cups peeled, finely grated tart apples
½ cup chopped walnuts

Preheat over to 350°. Sift together flour, baking powder, salt cinnamon and nutmeg. Cream together butter and sugar. Beat in eggs. Stir in alternately, flour mixture and apples. Add nuts. Pour into well greased and floured 9x5x3-inch loaf pan and bake 1 hour. Cool for 10 to 15 minutes before removing from pan.

Yield — 1 loaf.

PEAR NUT BREAD

1 cup pecans
4 ounces cream cheese, softened
1 Tablespoon vegetable oil
¾ cup plus 5 Tablespoons sugar
2 eggs
1 teaspoon lemon juice
1 cup chopped fresh pears
1 cup flour
2 teaspoons baking powder
¼ teaspoon salt
3 Tablespoons pear nectar
1 Tablespoon fresh lemon juice

Butter (unsalted) and flour an 8½x4½x2½-inch loaf pan.

Preheat oven to 350°. Spread pecans in ungreased baking pan. Bake until pecans are slightly toasted, about 8 minutes. Cool and grind in blender. Beat cream cheese and vegetable oil in large mixing bowl. Gradually beat in ¾ cup plus 2 Tablespoons of the sugar until well blended. Beat in eggs, one at a time, blending well after each addition, until mixture is light and fluffy. Stir in pears, pecans and 1 teaspoon lemon juice. Sift flour, baking powder and salt into small bowl. Fold into cream cheese mixture until just combined. Pour into pan, and bake for 1 hour.

While bread is baking, combine pear nectar, lemon juice and remaining 3 Tablespoons sugar, in a heavy saucepan, cook until sugar is melted. When bread is done, pour glaze over loaf in pan while bread is hot. Cool in pan on wire rack.

Yield — 1 loaf.

FRESH CRANBERRY BREAD

3 cups sifted flour
3 teaspoons baking powder
1½ teaspoons salt
½ teaspoon soda
½ cup shortening
1½ cups sugar
2 large eggs
¾ cup fresh orange juice
1½ Tablespoons grated orange rind
¾ cup chopped nuts
2½ cups fresh cranberries, coarsely chopped

Preheat oven to 350°.

Sift together flour, baking powder and salt. Measure shortening into mixing bowl, add soda, mix well. Gradually blend in sugar. Beat in eggs one at a time. Add flour mixture alternately with orange juice. Stir in orange rind, nuts and cranberries. Turn batter into a well-greased, lightly floured 9x5x3-inch loaf pan. Bake for 1½ hours.

Yield — 1 loaf.

BUTTERMILK NUT BREAD

1 cup firmly packed brown sugar
1 egg, well beaten
2 Tablespoons melted butter
2 cups sifted flour
½ teaspoon baking soda
¾ teaspoon baking powder
¼ teaspoon salt
1 cup buttermilk
1 cup coarsely chopped nuts
1 cup chopped dates

Preheat oven to 350°. Add sugar to beaten egg and beat until light. Add melted butter and blend. Add buttermilk and sifted dry ingredients alternately. Stir just enough to blend. Add dates and nuts. Bake in a 9x5x3-inch greased loaf pan for 1 hour.

Yield — 1 loaf.

CHRISTMAS DATE-NUT BREAD

1½ cups flour
1½ cups sugar
1 teaspoon baking powder
1 teaspoon salt
2 pounds fresh pitted dates, halved
2 cups walnut pieces
5 eggs
1 teaspoon vanilla

Preheat oven to 325°.

Sift together the flour, sugar, baking powder, and salt. Add dates and walnuts and stir until coated.

Beat eggs well, add vanilla and blend into fruit and flour mixture.

Put into 3 or 4 small well-greased loaf pans and bake for one hour.

This may be made well in advance, as it freezes beautifully.

PUMPKIN BREAD

2⅔ cups sugar
⅔ cup shortening
4 eggs, well beaten
2 cups canned pumpkin
⅔ cup water
3½ cups flour
½ teaspoon baking powder
2 teaspoons baking soda
1½ teaspoons salt
1 teaspoon cinnamon
½ teaspoon cloves
⅔ cup chopped nuts
⅔ cup chopped dates

Preheat oven to 350°.

Cream sugar and shortening. Add eggs, pumpkin and water, mix well.

Sift flour, baking powder, baking soda, salt, cinnamon, and cloves. Blend in nuts and dates and add to pumpkin mixture. Pour batter into two greased 9 x 5 x 3-inch loaf pans.

Bake for 1 hour and 15 minutes.

Yield — 2 loaves.

SUNNY ORANGE MUFFINS

1 slightly beaten egg
¼ cup sugar
½ cup orange juice
2 Tablespoons salad oil
2 cups packaged biscuit mix
½ cup orange marmalade
½ cup chopped pecans
½ cup sugar
½ teaspoon cinnamon
1½ Tablespoons flour
¼ teaspoon nutmeg
1 Tablespoon margarine

Combine first four ingredients, add biscuit mix and beat for 30 seconds. Stir in marmalade and pecans. Grease muffin pans and fill 2/3 full. Combine sugar, flour, cinnamon and nutmeg, cut in margarine till crumbly and sprinkle over batter. Bake at 350° for 20 minutes.

Yield: 12 muffins.

ALMOND DANISH PASTRY

This pastry freezes well.

First Crust:
1 cup flour
½ cup butter
3 Tablespoons water

Mix well and divide in half. Shape in two wide strips on ungreased cookie sheet.

Second Crust:
1 cup water
½ cup butter
1 cup flour
3 eggs

Boil water and butter, add flour and beat. Add eggs one at a time, beating well after each. Spread over first crust. Bake one hour at 350° and cool. Frost and cover frosting with toasted slivered almonds.

Frosting:
4 ounces cream cheese
8 ounces confectioner's sugar
½ teaspoon almond extract

BUTTERHORN PASTRY

These freeze very well.

1 cup margarine
12 ounces cottage cheese
2 cups flour
Dash of salt

Cream margarine and cottage cheese. Add flour and salt and mix well. Refrigerate 4 hours.

Preheat over to 350°. Divide dough into 3 parts. Roll each part in a 12-inch circle on a floured board. Cut circle in 12 wedges. Roll into butterhorn, starting roll at wide edge and rolling to a point. Place on greased cookie sheet and bake 30 to 40 minutes until light brown. Frost when still warm.

Circles of dough may be sprinkled with bits of candied fruit or nuts before rolling up horns, to vary taste.

Frosting:
1 cup powdered sugar
1 Tablespoon butter
¼ teaspoon vanilla
2 Tablespoons milk

Beat all ingredients together until smooth. Brush on rolls with a pastry brush.

MINCEMEAT COFFEE RING

2 cups sifted flour
¾ cup sugar
2½ teaspoons baking powder
½ teaspoon salt
⅓ cup shortening
1 egg, well beaten
½ cup milk
¾ cup moist mincemeat

Preheat oven to 375°.

Sift flour, sugar, salt and baking powder together into bowl. Cut in shortening with pastry blender until mixture resembles cornmeal. Blend egg, milk and mincemeat and add to dry ingredients. Stir until evenly moistened. Turn batter into well-greased 1½-quart ring mold or 8-inch-square pan, and bake for 30 minutes. Cool about 10 minutes. Remove from mold and drizzle with glaze while still warm.

Yield — 1 9-inch ring.

Glaze:
2 Tablespoons butter or margarine
3 Tablespoons hot milk
1 cup sifted powdered sugar
⅛ teaspoon salt

Combine butter and hot milk. Stir until butter is melted. Gradually add to powdered sugar and salt. Stir until smooth.

ANGEL BUNS

5 cups all-purpose flour
3 teaspoons baking powder
1 teaspoon salt
1 teaspoon baking soda
¼ cup sugar
1 cup shortening
1 package dry yeast
2 Tablespoons warm water
2 cups buttermilk
½ cup margarine

Preheat oven to 400°.

Sift together flour, baking powder, salt, soda and sugar. Cut in shortening. Dissolve yeast in warm water. Add with buttermilk to dry ingredients, mixing well. Turn out on floured board. Roll to ¼-inch thickness. Melt margarine in an 11x17-inch baking sheet. Cut out rolls with a 2½-inch biscuit cutter. Dip in melted butter, fold in half and place in rows in baking pan. Bake for 15 to 20 minutes.

Yield — 4½ to 5 dozen.

GERMAN PANCAKE

4 Tablespoons butter
½ cup flour
½ cup milk
½ teaspoon salt
4 eggs

Preheat oven to 400°. Melt butter in 10-inch oven-proof skillet. Combine flour, milk and salt in mixing bowl; add eggs one at a time, whipping after each addition. Pour mixture into skillet and cook over medium heat until bottom is golden brown. Loosen from bottom of pan. Make a criss-cross slash with knife through pancake, and place in oven. Bake until puffed and golden brown, 12 to 15 minutes. Serve pancake with lemon slices, confectioner's sugar and syrup.

Serves 2 generously

SIRNIKI

These Russian pancakes are an airy delight.

2 large eggs, separated
4 ounces cream cheese, softened
1 Tablespoon sugar
½ teaspoon salt
1 cup small curd cream-style cottage cheese
½ cup fork-stirred all-purpose flour
4 Tablespoons butter
Sour cream

With a spoon beat the egg yolks with the cream cheese, sugar and salt until blended; stir in the cottage cheese, add the flour and stir until it is blended. With a clean beater, beat the egg whites until stiff; fold into the cheese mixture. In a 10-inch skillet (preferably non-stick) over moderate heat, heat 2 Tablespoons of the butter; add the batter, dropping it by rounded Tablespoons, well apart. Brown on bottom sides *2 or 3 minutes*. Turn and brown top sides 2 to 3 minutes. Keep warm while frying remaining batter. Serve with sour cream and tart jam or jelly.

Makes 20 to 24

GOUGERE AUX FINES HERBES

½ cup butter
1 cup water
1 cup all-purpose flour
4 eggs
1 teaspoon dry mustard
½ teaspoon thyme
½ teaspoon oregano
1 teaspoon chervil
2 Tablespoons chopped parsley
½ teaspoon basil
1 teaspoon salt
¼ teaspoon cayenne
1½ cups grated Swiss cheese

Cut butter into pieces; place in saucepan with water and bring to boil; when butter is melted remove pan from heat and add flour all at once. Beat vigorously until smooth paste forms. Return to medium heat and beat until paste is shiny, about 1 minute. Remove from heat.

Make a well in paste; break 1 egg into well and beat vigorously until thoroughly blended; proceed with remaining 3 eggs, 1 egg at a time. Beat in mustard, thyme, oregano, chervil, parsley, basil, salt and cayenne. Fold in grated cheese.

Preheat oven to 450°. Lightly grease large baking sheet, 11x18x1-inch. Sprinkle lightly with flour. With finger, using round, 7-inch cake pan as guide, trace 7-inch circles in flour. Drop cheese-egg mixture by Tablespoons to form rings. Smooth each ring with rubber spatula.

Place in oven and bake 12 minutes; turn oven down to 325° and bake additional 30 minutes. Remove from oven; serve hot or cold, breaking chunks of gougere off as you would French bread, or slicing with knife, if preferred.

MEXICAN SPOON BREAD

1 cup yellow cornmeal
1 teaspoon salt
½ teaspoon baking soda
¾ cup milk
⅓ cup cooking oil
2 eggs, beaten
1 pound can cream style corn
1 4-ounce can chopped green chiles, drained
1½ cups shredded sharp Cheddar cheese.

Preheat oven to 350°.

Combine cornmeal, salt and baking soda. Mix well. Stir in milk and oil; mix well. Add eggs and corn; mix well. Spoon half of the mixture into a greased 1½ quart casserole. Sprinkle half of the chiles on top, than half of the cheese. Repeat layers, ending with cheese. Bake uncovered about 45 minutes or until toothpick inserted in center comes out clean.

Serves 6

CHURROS

1 cup water
6 Tablespoons butter
⅛ teaspoon salt
1 cup all-purpose flour
3 eggs
¼ teaspoon cinnamon or nutmeg
1 cup powdered sugar
Peanut oil for frying

Bring water to a boil in a 2-quart saucepan. Add butter and salt. Heat until butter is melted. Add flour all at once; remove from heat. Beat until mixture is smooth and is the consistency of mashed potatoes. Beat in one egg at a time. When smooth beat in cinnamon or nutmeg.

Turn mixture into a pastry bag fitted with a star tip. Pour oil 1-inch deep into a 10-inch skillet. Heat to 370°. Squeeze dough directly into hot oil, making churros about 8 inches long. Cook 3 or 4 at a time until a deep golden brown; turn occasionally. Drain over skillet, then on paper towels.

Sift powdered sugar over churros. Serve immediately.

Makes 16 churros.

eggs and chesse

GREEN ENCHILADAS

- 1 dozen corn tortillas
- ½ cup cooking oil
- 3 cups shredded Monterey Jack cheese
- ¾ cup chopped onion
- 4 Tablespoons butter or margarine
- ¼ cup all-purpose flour
- 1 14½-ounce can chicken broth
- 1 cup sour cream
- 1 4-ounce can diced green chiles

Soften tortillas in hot oil one at a time. Place 3 Tablespoons of cheese and 1 Tablespoon of onion on each tortilla; roll up. Place seam side down in an 11 x 7½ x 1½″ baking dish.

In a saucepan, melt butter or margarine; blend in flour. Add chicken broth all at once; cook and stir until mixture thickens and bubbles. Stir in sour cream and green chiles. Heat through but do not boil. Pour over tortillas in baking dish. Bake in 425° oven for 20 minutes.

Sprinkle remaining cheese over top, return to oven for 5 minutes or until cheese melts. Serve with additional sour cream and salsa.

Serves 4

FRITATA

This makes a delightful brunch or luncheon dish.

⅓ cup chopped green pepper
⅓ cup chopped red pepper
1½ cups sliced mushrooms
1½ cups chopped zucchini
¾ cup chopped onion
1 large clove garlic, minced
3 Tablespoons cooking oil
6 eggs, beaten
¼ cup light cream
1 pound cream cheese, diced
1½ cups shredded Cheddar cheese
2 cups cubed white bread
1 teaspoon salt
¼ teaspoon pepper

Preheat oven to 350°.

Sauté peppers, mushrooms, zucchini, onion and garlic in oil until zucchini is crisp-tender. Cool slightly.

Beat eggs with cream. Add cream cheese, cheddar cheese, bread, salt, pepper and vegetables. Mix well. Pour into greased 10-inch spring-form pan. Bake for one hour or until set in center. Cool 10 minutes before cutting, or serve at room temperature.

Serves 8

ZUCCHINI QUICHE

Salt
2 cups chopped, unpeeled zucchini
1 small onion, chopped
1½ Tablespoons butter
1 Tablespoon flour
3 eggs, lightly beaten
1 cup milk or half and half
1½ cups shredded Swiss cheese
½ teaspoon oregano
Pinch of basil
Salt and pepper to taste
1 9″ unbaked pie shell

Preheat oven to 400°.

Sprinkle salt over zucchini and let stand 30 minutes. Rinse, drain and blot dry with paper towel. Set aside.

Sauté the onion in butter; add zucchini and flour and cook 1 minute.

Beat eggs and milk in bowl; add cheese, seasonings and zucchini and mix well. Pour into unbaked pastry shell. Place in oven and immediately reduce heat to 350°, bake for 1 hour or until quiche is set. Let stand 15 minutes before cutting.

Serves 6

FRENCH FRIED ONION QUICHE

9″ deep-dish pastry shell
1½ cups shredded Swiss cheese
1 3-ounce can French fried onions
3 eggs, slightly beaten
1½ cups half and half
½ teaspoon salt
⅛ teaspoon pepper
Paprika
Dairy sour cream

Preheat oven to 400°.

If using frozen pastry shell, let stand at room temperature 10 minutes. Do not prick the pastry shell, bake 7 minutes. Remove from oven. Reduce oven temperature to 375°.

Sprinkle first the cheese and then 1⅓ cups French fried onions in the pastry shell. In a medium bowl, combine eggs, half and half, salt and pepper. Beat with a fork or whisk until mixed well but not frothy. Pour egg mixture over onions and cheese in pastry shell. Sprinkle with paprika. Bake 45 minutes or until a knife inserted off-center comes out clean. Let stand 10 minutes before serving.

Top with sour cream and remaining onions.

Serves 6

24 HOUR WINE AND CHEESE OMELET

1 large loaf French or Italian bread, broken into small pieces
6 Tablespoons unsalted butter
¾ pound Swiss cheese, shredded
½ pound Monterey Jack cheese, shredded
½ to 1 cup bacon, or salami, or shrimp or green pepper (optional)
16 eggs
3¼ cups milk
½ cup dry white wine
4 large green onions, minced
1 Tablespoon Dijon mustard
¼ teaspoon pepper
⅛ teaspoon cayenne
1½ cups sour cream
1 cup freshly grated Parmesan cheese

Butter two shallow 3-quart (9″ x 13″) baking dishes. Spread bread over bottom and drizzle with butter. Sprinkle with two cheeses and optional ingredients you wish to use.

Beat together eggs, milk, wine, green onion, mustard, pepper and cayenne until foamy. Pour over cheese. Cover dishes with foil, crimping edges. Refrigerate overnight or up to 24 hours.

Remove from refrigerator 30 minutes before baking. Bake covered in preheated 325° about 1 hour. Uncover, spread with sour cream and sprinkle with Parmesan and bake uncovered until lightly browned, about 10 minutes.

Serves 12

FETTUCINE ALLA FRANCESCA

2 Tablespoons butter
2 Tablespoons olive oil
1 small onion, chopped
1 clove garlic, minced
2 cups broccoli flowerettes
½ cup chopped ham
½ pound Fettucine, cooked al dente
Parmesan cheese, grated
Parsley, minced

Sauce
1 cup half and half or part heavy cream
¼ cup grated Parmesan cheese
1 egg yolk
Dash of nutmeg
Salt and pepper to taste

In butter and olive oil, saute onion, garlic and broccoli. Add ham.

For sauce, combine all ingredients in saucepan and cook, stirring constantly, until creamy. If too thick, add more cream. Add sauce to broccoli mixture.

Toss with Fettucine and top with grated Parmesan and parsley.

Any combination of vegetables can be used, e.g. zucchini, peas, asparagus, mushrooms, fresh tomatoes.

Serves 4 to 6

LENTIL CASSEROLE

1⅓ cups dried lentils
1 onion, finely chopped
1 Tablespoon margarine
2 garlic cloves, minced
2 cups scraped and grated carrots
2 cups canned tomatoes, drained
½ small green bell pepper, seeded and chopped
1 teaspoon salt
½ teaspoon freshly ground black pepper
¼ teaspoon crushed dried marjoram
¼ teaspoon crushed dried thyme
1½ cups shredded Monterey Jack cheese

Place lentils in water to cover in a saucepan and cook approximately 1 hour.

Sauté onion and garlic in margarine until clear and tender.

Combine onion, garlic, lentils and remaining ingredients in casserole. Sprinkle cheese on top. Bake or microwave until bubbly.

Serves 8

WILD RICE PARTY DISH

¼ pound butter
1 cup raw wild rice
½ cup slivered almonds
2 Tablespoons chopped onions
½ pound sliced mushrooms
1 teaspoon salt
2 Tablespoons sherry
3 cups chicken broth

In heavy frying pan, cook all but broth until rice is well coated, stirring frequently.

Place in casserole with broth. Cover. Refrigerate or freeze.

When ready to serve, return to room temperature, then bake at 325° for 1 hour.

May stand awhile, if necessary, after cooking.

Serves 4

CHINESE RICE

Excellent served with grilled pork chops.

4 slices bacon
1 medium onion, diced
½ green pepper, diced or cut in strips
1 cup raw rice
1 10¾-ounce can beef consommé
1 10¾-ounce can water
Salt and pepper to taste

Fry bacon, drain, reserving drippings, and crumble.

Sauté onion and green pepper in drippings until soft. Add rice, consommé, water and seasonings. Cover and cook over low heat until liquid is absorbed, or bake at 350° for 45 to 55 minutes.

Serves 6 to 8

EXOTIC RICE CASSEROLE

This is an unusual and delicious rice dish.

- 2 cups dried apricots
- 1 cup white raisins
- 2 cups raw rice
- 1 cup minced onion
- ½ cup chopped green pepper
- ½ cup butter
- 1 cup toasted almonds

Cover fruit with water; soak ½ hour, drain and chop.

Cook rice according to package directions until tender.

Sauté onion and green pepper in butter. Add almonds, rice and fruit.

Bake in greased, 2-quart covered baking dish at 375° 30 minutes.

Serves 10

STUFFED ORANGES

4 medium-sized navel oranges
1 red sweet pepper
4 large black olives
1 cup cold cooked rice
¼ cup chopped green onion tops
½ teaspoon curry powder
2 Tablespoons oil
2 teaspoons wine vinegar
Salt to taste
Lettuce
4 large stuffed green olives

Cut a thick slice from the stem end of each orange. Carefully cut out the segments and remove the membrane, keeping the rind intact. Scrape out the orange cases to remove all seeds and membrane. Notch the edges with scissors or a sharp knife.

Cut pepper in half and remove seeds and all pithy tissue. Cut into short, julienne strips. Cut the orange sections and olives into fine dice and add to the peppers along with rice and onion tops.

Combine curry powder, oil, vinegar and salt. Pour over the orange and rice mixture and marinate 1 hour. Drain and spoon into the orange cases. Serve on lettuce. Garnish each with a stuffed green olive.

Serves 4

entrees

FAVORITE BEEF BURGUNDY

16 small white onions, peeled
6 slices lean bacon, diced
¼ cup butter
4 pounds beef, cut into 1½-inch cubes, fat trimmed off
¼ cup brandy
1½ teaspoons salt
¼ teaspoon pepper
2 cups dry red table wine
2 whole cloves garlic, peeled
2 cups small fresh mushrooms, whole or sliced
1½ cups water
1 or 2 springs parsley
1 celery top
1 carrot, quartered
1 bay leaf
1 teaspoon thyme
6 Tablespoons flour
½ cup cold water

Brown onions with bacon and butter in a heavy skillet. Remove onions and bacon with a slotted spoon and set aside. Add meat to pan and brown well on all sides. Pour brandy over beef and set aflame, tilting pan to keep flame going as long as possible. Sprinkle meat with salt and pepper. Add red wine, garlic, mushrooms, the 1½ cups water, onions and bacon. Make a bouquet garni by tying together in a piece of cheesecloth, the parsley, celery top, carrot, bay leaf, and thyme. Add bouquet garni. Cover and simmer for about 1½ hours, or until the meat is tender.

Lift beef, mushrooms and onions out of the pan with a slotted spoon; arrange in a covered 3-quart casserole. Strain the liquid through a sieve, discarding bouquet garni, garlic and bacon. Mix flour to a smooth paste with the ½ cup cold water; stir into meat stock and cook, stirring until gravy is thick and smooth. Pour gravy over meat and serve immediately or refrigerate and reheat, covered in a moderate oven for about 35 minutes, or until hot and bubbly.

Serves 8 to 10

LA BOEUF DE WELLINGTON

4½ pounds beef tenderloin roast
Butter
1½ teaspoons salt
½ teaspoon black seasoned pepper
1 Tablespoon clarified butter
½ pound fresh mushrooms, chopped
2 Tablespoons finely minced onions
1 Tablespoon finely chopped shallots
2 ounces lean ham, finely chopped
¼ cup Madeira wine
1 large can goose liver pâté with truffles
Salt and pepper to taste
2 packages frozen patty shells, thawed

Madeira Sauce
3 Tablespoons flour
¼ cup reserved pan drippings
½ teaspoon salt
Pepper to taste
½ cup Madeira

Spread a layer of butter on meat and season with salt and pepper. Roast in a preheated 450° oven until rare or medium, to your preference. Reserve ¼ cup drippings. Cool, then place roast in refrigerator. This can be done a day or two before serving.

Squeeze excess moisture from mushrooms. Sauté mushrooms, shallots and onions in butter until just brown; then add ham and wine. Simmer until liquid is reduced and mixture becomes thick. Season to taste with salt and pepper. May be refrigerated a day or two before using.

If meat is prepared ahead of time, allow one hour for meat to come to room temperature.

Spread the pâté over the surface of the entire roast, then spread the top of the meat with the mushroom mixture.

Lightly flour a pastry board and roll the patty shell dough ⅛ inch thick into an oblong shape. It should be large enough to completely cover the entire piece of beef. Place the beef on the pastry and fold the pastry around it. Trim off any excess and seal any openings. Put the sealed edge underneath and decorate as you wish. Brush the dough with beaten egg white and place on a baking tray. Prick here and there so that the steam will escape. Bake in preheated 425° oven until pastry is browned, about 10 minutes.

Serve with Madeira Sauce. To make sauce, combine flour and the pan drippings and stir over medium heat. Stir constantly and add the Madeira gradually. Stir in the water and continue to stir while cooking until thickened.

Serves 6 to 8

FILETS ROYAL

8 beef tenderloins
1 4-ounce can goose liver paté

Stuffing
1 cup sliced mushrooms
1 bunch green onions, sliced
2 Tablespoons butter

Sauce
2 Tablespoons butter
3 Tablespoons flour
½ cup milk
1 cup whipping cream
½ cup brandy
¼ cup chives

Butterfly tenderloins and brown in heavy skillet over high flame until almost done. Fill with stuffing mixture and slice of paté, then refry and top with sauce.

To make stuffing, sauté mushrooms and green onions in butter.

To make sauce, melt butter in pan, stir in flour until smooth and blend in milk, cream and brandy. Simmer, stirring constantly, until sauce thickens.

Serves 8

STRIP STEAK DELUXE

2½ pounds steak
1 large onion, chopped
4 Tablespoons butter
Flour
3 Tablespoons vinegar
1 teaspoon dry mustard
½ teaspoon paprika
1 teaspoon thyme
1 teaspoon salt
1 teaspoon pepper
½ teaspoon cayenne
⅔ cup water
⅓ cup half and half

With a sharp knife, slice steak diagonally into ¼-inch strips. In a heavy skillet brown the chopped onion in 2 Tablespoons butter. Dredge the steak slices in flour, add them to the onion butter, and sauté gently until brown. In a saucepan melt 2 Tablespoons butter, stir in 1 Tablespoons flour, the vinegar and mustard, paprika, thyme, salt, pepper and cayenne. Add water and half and half. Pour sauce over the steak, cover the skillet and simmer for about ½ hour.

Serves 4

CHUTNEY PEPPER STEAK

Spicy hot!

2 to 2½ pounds steak, 1½ to 2 inches thick
(top sirloin is best)
Cracked pepper
¼ cup butter
⅓ cup brandy
½ cup dry red wine
10-ounce jar chutney (peach or pineapple)

Trim meat of excess fat. Press pepper into both sides of meat. Let sit approximately one hour.

Melt butter in heavy skillet over medium heat. Sauté steak in butter 5 to 7 minutes on each side. Pour in brandy and flame. After flame dies, remove steak. Place wine and chutney in same skillet and heat through. Return steak to skillet and baste with sauce, continuing to cook to desired doneness.

Serves 4 to 6.

BARBECUED BEEF BRISKET

3 to 6 pound beef brisket
Liquid smoke
Celery salt
Onion salt
Garlic powder

Sauce
1⅓ cups catsup
½ cup vinegar
4 Tablespoons brown sugar
1 large onion, chopped
2 cloves garlic
4 Tablespoons margarine
2 teaspoons Worcestershire sauce
2 teaspoons dry mustard

Rub the brisket with liquid smoke and seasonings, using enough of each to cover brisket well. Place in covered roaster, directly on bottom, add a little water and cook for 5 hours at 275°.

After 4 hours, remove cover, score meat with knife, and add barbecue sauce. Continue cooking 1 hour longer.

For sauce, combine all ingredients and simmer for a few minutes.

Serves
10 to 12

GREEN CHILI STEW

This is delicious served with warm tortillas.

3 pounds stewing meat, cubed
1 Tablespoon cooking oil
1 cup water
1 4-ounce can chopped green chiles
1 onion, chopped
4 tomatoes, peeled
1½ teaspoons salt
⅔ teaspoon comino (cumin)
¼ teaspoon oregano
1 10¾-ounce can bean with bacon soup

Brown meat in skillet in oil. Add water to meat; cover and simmer until tender, 2 or 3 hours.

Add all other ingredients and simmer 30 minutes.

Can be cooked in crock pot 6 to 8 hours.

Serves
4 to 6

CASSOULET

1 pound sirloin tip steak, cut in cubes
½ pound lean pork, cut in cubes
4 ounces cooking oil
1 whole garlic clove
½ pound fresh mushrooms, sliced
2 Tablespoons butter
Dry white wine
2 Tablespoons catsup
1 to 2 large onions, chopped
2 Tablespoons oil
1 bay leaf
8 peppercorns
1 16-ounce can pinto beans
1 16-ounce can kidney beans

Saute meats in oil with garlic until tender and brown.

Meanwhile, sauté mushrooms in butter.

When meat is brown, add enough wine to cover. Add mushrooms and catsup, cover and let simmer for 35 minutes, adding more wine if necessary.

Sauté onions in oil with bay leaf and peppercorns until golden.

Combine onions with beans and add to meat mixture. Transfer to a casserole and bake at 300° for 1 hour.

Serves
4 to 6

BREWERY GULCH BEEF, BEANS AND BONES

2 cups fresh pinto beans
1 ham hock (may substitute pork neck bones)
1 or 2 beef neck bones
1 medium onion, chopped
1 6-ounce can tomato sauce
1 teaspoon marjoram
1 teaspoon comino (cumin)
¼ teaspoon cayenne pepper
1 Tablespoon prepared mustard
1 Tablespoon Worcestershire sauce
1 to 2 teaspoons salt
3 garlic cloves, minced
1 to 2 Tablespoons chili powder

Wash beans and place in crock pot. Add 6 cups of water, ham hocks and neck bones and cook at least 8 hours.

Remove bones and add remaining ingredients. Cook another 8 hours.

Serves 6 to 8

CHILI CASSEROLE

1 large onion, chopped
1 green pepper, chopped
¼ cup oil
2 pounds ground beef
2 teaspoons chili powder
½ teaspoon oregano
¼ teaspoon garlic powder
2 teaspoons salt
¼ teaspoon pepper
3½ cups red chili sauce
2½ cups canned whole kernel corn, drained
1 4½-ounce can pitted black olives
10 soft corn tortillas
½ cup oil
1 pound Tillamook cheese, grated
Chopped green onions
Sour cream

Sauté onions and pepper in oil. Stir in beef and cook until meat loses red color. Add seasonings, chili sauce, corn and olives.

Cut or tear tortillas and fry quickly in hot oil until just soft.

Place double layer of tortillas in bottom of 9″ x 13″ casserole; alternate layers of tortillas, meat mixture and cheese, ending with cheese. Bake uncovered at 350° for 45 minutes.

Garnish with green onions and sour cream.

Serves 6 to 8

CLAIRE'S LASAGNE

1 pound sweet Italian sausage links
1 pound ground chuck
Salt and freshly ground pepper
½ pound mushrooms, chopped
1 teaspoon chopped garlic
Marinara sauce (see below)
Ricotta filling (see below)
3 Tablespoons butter
3 Tablespoons flour
1 cup milk
1¼ cups heavy cream
¼ teaspoon nutmeg
1 pound lasagne noodles
½ pound mozzarella cheese, cut into cubes
½ cup freshly grated Parmesan cheese

Marinara Sauce

½ cup olive oil
4 cups coarsely chopped onions
1 cup sliced carrots
4 cloves garlic, finely minced
8 cups canned Italian plum tomatoes drained
Salt and pepper to taste
¼ pound butter, melted
2 teaspoons dried oregano
2 teaspoons dried basil or 2 Tablespoons fresh basil

Ricotta

1 pound Ricotta cheese
3 eggs
1 cup grated Parmesan cheese or ½ cup Parmesan and ½ cup Pecorino
2 Tablespoons chopped parsely
Salt and pepper to taste

Marinara Sauce: Heat oil in large pot and add onion, garlic and carrots. Cook, stirring until golden brown. Puree tomatoes in blender; add to vegetables and salt and pepper to taste. Partly cover and simmer 15 minutes. Blend in blender and return to pot. Add remaining ingredients, partly cover and simmer 30 minutes longer.

In large skillet, cook sausages until done. Drain, pouring off most of the fat, and set meat aside. In same skillet, brown the meat in the sausage drippings, adding salt and pepper to taste, breaking up lumps in the meat. Add mushrooms and garlic, stirring frequently, until meat loses its red color. Continue cooking until meat starts to brown.

Skin the sausages and slice thin. Mix with cooked meat and add to marinara sauce. Simmer, partly covered, about 45 minutes, stirring occasionally.

While sauce cooks, melt 3 Tablespoons butter in pan. Stir in flour with wire whisk. When blended, add milk. When thickened, stir in cream; add salt, pepper and nutmeg. Stir this sauce into meat sauce.

Ricotta: Mix all ingredients together.

Cook lasagne noodles according to directions on package. Drain immediately and rinse in cold water.

Assemble in 9x13-inch baking dish as follows: sauce, noodles, ricotta, marinara sauce, mozzarella cheese, parmesan cheese, and repeat. Bake at 350° for 45 minutes, or until piping hot and bubbling throughout.

This freezes very well and it's wise to prepare 3 or 4 recipes at a time.

ENCHILADA CASSEROLE

13 ounce package corn chips
3 cups shredded sharp Cheddar cheese
2 cups sour cream
2 15½-ounce cans chili with beans
2 15½-ounce chili without beans
2 cups tomato sauce
3 cups enchilada sauce
2 Tablespoons chopped onion
1 16-ounce can chopped black olives
1 4-ounce can chopped green chiles

Reserve 1 cup corn chips, 1 cup cheese and 2 cups sour cream.

Place remaining ingredients in a 4 quart casserole, mixing well, and bake at 350° for 30 minutes.

Spread sour cream on top and garnish with remaining corn chips and cheese. Bake for 5 minutes longer.

Serves 8 to 10

MARZETTI

2 pounds lean ground beef
2 medium onions, sliced
1 green pepper, chopped
Handful of chopped parsley
1 clove garlic, minced
1 pound fresh mushrooms, sliced
¼ cup butter
3 Tablespoons Worcestershire sauce
2 10¾-ounce cans tomato soup
1 12-ounce can tomato paste
1 12-ounce package wide noodles
10 ounces sharp Cheddar cheese, grated
Salt and pepper to taste

Sauté meat until light brown. Remove meat from pan and sauté onions, green pepper, parsley and garlic in meat drippings. Combine with meat.

Sauté mushrooms quickly in butter. Do not allow to brown. Combine with meat mixture.

Add Worcestershire sauce, soup and tomato paste to meat mixture.

Cook noodles and drain. Arrange half the noodles in the bottom of a greased 9″ x 12″ x 2″ casserole. Follow with a third of the cheese, then half the meat mixture. Repeat with remaining ingredients, saving a layer of cheese for the top.

Bake at 350° 1 hour. Can be prepared ahead and frozen. Allow to completely defrost before baking.

Serves 10.

MEXICAN SPAGHETTI

2 pounds lean ground beef
1 onion, chopped
2 pound jar spaghetti sauce with mushrooms
2 4-ounce cans diced green chiles
⅛ teaspoon pepper
1 teaspoon salt
1 teaspoon chili powder
1 12-ounce package spaghetti
1 pound shredded longhorn cheese

Brown and drain ground beef. Add onions and cook several minutes. Add spaghetti sauce, chiles, salt and pepper. Sprinkle with chili powder and simmer on low heat 30 minutes.

Meanwhile, cook spaghetti until tender and drain. Pour spaghetti back into pan and pour sauce into it. Mix with two large forks until well mixed.

Layer half of spaghetti mixture into 9 x 13-inch casserole. Layer half the cheese over that. Pour in the rest of the spaghetti and cover with remaining cheese. Cover and refrigerate.

Bake at 350° for 40 minutes.

Serves 8

CHILI WITH BEANS

5 Tablespoons corn oil
1 cup coarsely chopped onions
4 cloves garlic, chopped fine
½ cup diced green pepper
2 pounds coarsely ground beef
4 cups peeled, quartered tomatoes
4 cups freshly cooked kidney beans
1 teaspoon salt
4 Tablespoons chili powder
1 cup boiling water
1 Tablespoon red wine vinegar (optional)
1 Tablespoon brown sugar (optional)

Heat corn oil in Dutch oven. Sauté onions, garlic and green pepper until onions are translucent. Add beef and brown.

Add remaining ingredients except water. Cover and simmer for at least 1 hour. Add 1 cup water plus extra water if a thinner consistency is desired.

For a more authentic Mexican taste, add the vinegar and sugar. Overnight storage and reheating will blend and ripen the flavors. Freezes beautifully.

Serves 8

MEXICAN CASSEROLE

This is a microwave dish.

- 1½ pounds ground beef
- ½ cup chopped green pepper
- ½ cup chopped onion
- 1¼-ounce package taco seasoning
- 1 8-ounce can tomato sauce
- 1 6-ounce can tomato paste
- ½ cup sliced ripe olives
- ¼ cup water
- ½ teaspoon chili powder
- 1 cup sour cream
- 2 eggs
- ¼ teaspoon pepper
- 4 8-inch flour tortillas
- 2 cups broken corn chips
- 2 cups shredded Monterey Jack cheese

Crumble beef in 2 quart casserole; add green pepper and onions. Microwave at High 3 to 5 minutes or until meat loses its pink color. Stir and drain. Mix in taco seasoning, tomato sauce and paste, olives, water and chili powder. Microwave at Medium 10 to 15 minutes, or until thickened.

Blend sour cream, eggs and pepper in a small bowl.

Place 2 tortillas on bottom of 12 x 8-inch dish. Top with half meat mixture and half sour cream mixture. Repeat. Sprinkle with corn chips then cheese. Microwave at Medium 3 to 5 minutes or until cheese melts. Let stand 5 minutes.

Serves
4 to 6

SPAGHETTI SAUCE

This freezes very well.

¼ cup olive oil
2 slices bacon, chopped
1 onion, chopped
7 cloves garlic, minced
2 6-ounce cans tomato paste
2 28-ounce cans tomato puree
2 28-ounce cans Italian tomatoes
  chopped slightly
1 cup red wine
2 cups water
1 teaspoon salt
½ teaspoon pepper
¼ cup chopped parsley
1 Tablespoon chopped basil
1½ to 2 pounds ground beef

Sauté onion and bacon in olive oil. When almost brown, add garlic and brown. Add tomato paste and cook on low heat 2 or 3 minutes. Add all remaining ingredients except meat and simmer approximately 2 hours.

Brown ground beef, drain fat and add to sauce. Simmer at least 2 hours more, stirring occasionally.

BEV'S SUPER SPAGHETTI SAUCE

¾ cup olive oil
2 large garlic cloves, finely chopped
2 large onions, finely chopped
1 cup chopped parsley
1 large green pepper, chopped
1 cup chopped celery
1 small bay leaf
6-ounce can tomato paste
8-ounce can tomato sauce
1 24-ounce and 1 16-ounce can tomatoes, chopped
1 clove garlic, minced
1 Tablespoon oregano
1 Tablespoon basil
3 teaspoons salt
½ teaspoon pepper
Dash of cayenne pepper
1 Tablespoon sugar
¼ teaspoon baking soda
1½ pounds ground beef, browned

Sauté garlic and onions in olive oil. Add parsley, green pepper, celery, and bay leaf and cook slowly until tender. Add tomato paste, rinsing can with hot water and adding to mixture; tomato sauce, and tomatoes. Simmer slowly until sauce is thick and glossy. Add garlic, oregano, basil and 1 teaspoon salt during cooking.

Toward end of cooking, add 2 teaspoons salt, peppers, sugar, soda and ground beef.

Serve over hot spaghetti.

Serves 8

SWEDISH MEATLOAF WITH SOUR CREAM DILL SAUCE

1½ cups soft bread crumbs
½ cup catsup
2 eggs, beaten
1 Tablespoon Worcestershire sauce
2 teaspoons salt
¼ teaspoon pepper
2 pounds lean ground beef
½ cup finely chopped onion
½ cup finely chopped dill pickle

Sour Cream Dill Sauce
1 cup sour cream
½ cup chopped dill pickle
½ cup dill pickle juice
¼ cup mayonnaise
1 Tablespoon flour

Combine bread crumbs, catsup, eggs, Worcestershire sauce, salt and pepper. Let stand for 5 minutes. Add meat, onion and pickle and mix well. Pack into a 9 x 5 x 3-inch loaf pan.

Bake in a 350° oven for 1 hour. Serve hot or cold with hot or cold Sour Cream Dill Sauce.

For sauce, combine ingredients and heat slowly, stirring constantly, until thickened. Serve hot with meat loaf. If cold sauce is desired, combine ingredients, omitting flour, and refrigerate until serving time. Makes 1¾ cups sauce.

Serves 8

VEAL AND WATER CHESTNUTS IN CREAM

1 cup butter
2½ pounds veal shoulder cut in 1½-inch cubes
1 medium onion, finely chopped
1 clove garlic, minced (optional)
Salt to taste
½ teaspoon MSG (optional)
¼ teaspoon freshly ground black pepper
1 pound fresh mushrooms, sliced
1 cup beef broth
2 8-ounce cans water chestnuts, drained and quartered
2 bay leaves
2 cups heavy cream
¼ cup brandy
¼ cup chopped parsley

Preheat oven to 375°.

Melt half the butter in an ovenproof casserole and sauté the veal lightly until gray. Remove the veal and sauté the onion and garlic, adding the salt, MSG and pepper. Return the veal to the casserole and remove from heat.

Melt remaining butter in a skillet and sauté the mushrooms. Add the mushrooms, beef broth, water chestnuts and bay leaves to the veal. Place in the oven and bake, covered, 1½ hours. (May be prepared ahead and refrigerated at this point.)

When ready to use, add the cream and simmer on top of the stove 15 to 20 minutes.

Just before serving, add the brandy and parsley. Reheat quickly and serve immediately.

Serves 6

PORK CHOP APPLEKRAUT

4 pork chops
Flour, salt and pepper to season
¼ cup cooking oil
1 16-ounce can sauerkraut, drained
1 medium onion, sliced
2 apples, cored and peeled
½ teaspoon caraway seed (optional)
⅓ cup brown sugar

Rub flour and seasonings into the chops. Brown in oil.

Combine remaining ingredients, place in a 2 quart cassserole and cover with chops. Bake, covered, 1 hour at 350° until done.

Serves 4

SAUSAGE TWICE WITH RICE

A different and slightly spicy taste makes this a nice addition to anyone's recipe file.

1 pound bulk sausage
1 pound smoked link sausage, sliced thin
1 cup green pepper, chopped
1 cup green olives, chopped
3 cups celery, coarsely chopped
2 3.5-ounce boxes chicken noodle soup mix
4½ cups boiling water
1 cup rice, uncooked
1 cup almonds, sliced

Brown sausage and drain. Add vegetables and set aside.

In large pan or Dutch oven combine soup mix, water and rice. Cover and simmer 20 minutes.

When barely tender, add sausage mixture and ¾ cup almonds. Stir well. Pour into greased 9 x 12-inch glass dish, sprinkle with remaining ¼ cup almonds and bake at 350° for 40 minutes.

Serves 8 to 10

POLISH POT PIE

This can be done on top of the stove or in the oven.

1 pound Polish sausage, cut in one inch cubes
4 large potatoes, peeled and sliced ½ inch thick
4 large onions, peeled and sliced ½ inch thick
1-pound can tomatoes, not drained
Salt and pepper to taste
3 Tablespoons sour cream

Combine sausage, potatoes, onions, tomatoes and seasonings. Cover and cook as follows: bake at 350° for 1½ hours; or cook on top of stove for 30 minutes. When tender, stir in sour cream.

Serves 4

CHINESE SAUSAGE RICE CASSEROLE

3 cups boiling water
2 envelopes dehydrated chicken noodle soup
½ cup raw long grain rice
1 pound ground sausage
1 large onion, sliced
1 cup bias cut celery
½ green pepper, bias cut
1 cup sliced and drained water chestnuts
Salt, pepper and sage to taste

Pour boiling water over soup and rice and let stand.

Crumble and cook sausage; drain, reserving a small amount of drippings. Sauté vegetables in oil. Combine all ingredients in casserole and bake at 325° for 1½ hours uncovered. Water may have to be added during cooking.

Serves 4 to 6.

REUBEN CASSEROLE

A sandwich in a dish!

1¾ cups sauerkraut, drained
½ pound cooked corned beef, thickly sliced
2 cups shredded Swiss cheese
3 Tablespoons Thousand Island dressing
2 medium tomatoes, peeled and sliced thin or
  2 cups canned tomatoes, drained and cut up
2 Tablespoons butter
1 cup fresh rye bread crumbs with caraway
¼ cup margarine

Place sauerkraut in buttered 1½-quart casserole. Top with corned beef, then Swiss cheese. Dab on dressing. Layer on tomatoes and dot with butter.

Sauté bread crumbs in margarine and spread over casserole. Bake at 425° for 30 minutes.

Serves 6

TARRAGON CHICKEN BREASTS

3 whole chicken breasts, skinned and split
6 Tablespoons butter
¼ cup puree of onion
2 teaspoons seasoned pepper
2 teaspoons seasoned salt
1 cup vermouth
1 cup whipping cream
3 teaspoons dried tarragon
3 Tablespoons Dijon mustard
1 cup grated Swiss cheese

Melt butter in large, heavy skillet; add chicken and sauté over medium-high heat on both sides until golden. Spread each breast with 2 teaspoons of onion puree; sprinkle with salt and pepper and pour vermouth around sides. Reduce heat, cover and cook gently 15 to 20 minutes, or until the breasts are tender. Remove chicken from skillet and keep warm.

Pour whipping cream into skillet and stir in tarragon and mustard. Simmer about 5 minutes to blend flavors then return breasts to skillet, turning to coat with sauce. Sprinkle with cheese and heat until cheese melts.

Serves
4 to 6

LAURA'S CHICKEN

3 whole chicken breasts, split and skinned
½ cup butter
1 heaping Tablespoon Spice Island chicken stock
Garlic salt to taste
Dill, fresh or dried

Melt butter and stir in chicken stock and garlic salt to taste. Marinate chicken breasts at least one hour, turning to coat evenly. Remove chicken and place in shallow baking dish; sprinkle generously with dill and bake in 350° oven for 1 hour, basting several times with seasoned butter.

Serves 6

CHICKEN DIABLO

This can be served as an entree or an hors d'oeuvres.

4 Tablespoons butter
½ cup honey
¼ cup Dijon mustard
1 teaspoon salt
1 teaspoon curry powder
3 whole chicken breasts, skinned, boned and split
or
1 whole chicken
or
24 wingettes (for hors d'oeuvres)
Sesame seeds

Melt butter and stir in honey, mustard, salt and curry powder. Pour over chicken and bake at 375° for 1 hour.

If using wingettes, dip in sesame seeds before baking.

Serves 6

CHICKEN PARMIGIANO

This tastes almost like veal, at a fraction of the price!

4 chicken breasts, boned
½ teaspoon salt (optional)
⅛ teaspoon pepper
1 egg
2 teaspoons water
⅓ cup grated Parmesan cheese
⅓ cup (or more) fine, dry bread crumbs
Garlic powder, parsley and paprika
¼ cup oil
2 or 3 Tablespoons finely chopped onion
1 6-ounce can tomato paste
2 cans water
salt
½ teaspoon basil
4 to 6 slices mozzarella, Swiss or Muenster cheese

Flatten chicken breasts by pounding lightly between sheets of wax paper. Sprinkle with salt and pepper. In shallow bowl lightly beat egg with 2 teaspoons water. On sheet of wax paper (or paper plate) combine Parmesan, bread crumbs, garlic powder, parsley and paprika. Dip chicken in egg, then in Parmesan mixture. In skillet brown chicken on both sides (taking care not to crowd) in oil. Remove chicken to baking dish. To skillet add onion and cook until tender. Stir in tomato paste, 2 cans water, salt and basil. Simmer 5 minutes, scraping up any browned bits from bottom of skillet. Pour most of sauce over chicken. Top with cheese. Pour remaining sauce over.

Bake at 350° for 20 to 25 minutes.

Serves 4

SWISS CHICKEN

¼ cup flour
1½ teaspoons salt
1 teaspoon paprika
5 whole chicken breasts, split, skinned and boned
¼ cup butter
2 Tablespoons cornstarch
1½ cups cream
¼ cup sherry
1 teaspoon lemon peel
1 Tablespoon lemon juice
1 cup grated Swiss cheese

Mix flour, salt and paprika and coat chicken. Brown lightly in butter. Add ¼ cup water and simmer covered until tender, about 40 minutes. Remove chicken to flat, oblong casserole.

Mix remaining ingredients except cheese in same skillet and heat until slightly thickened; pour over chicken. Bake uncovered at 350° for 30 minutes. Sprinkle with cheese and return to oven until cheese melts.

Freezes well.

Serves 6 to 8.

CHICKEN ROMANO

⅓ cup all-purpose flour
½ teaspoon salt
¼ teaspoon pepper
3 whole chicken breasts, split and skinned
2 Tablespoons melted shortening or vegetable oil
¼ cup minced onion
2 cups tomato juice
2 Tablespoons grated Romano cheese
1 Tablespoon sugar
½ teaspoon salt
½ teaspoon garlic salt
½ teaspoon whole oregano
¼ teaspoon basil leaves
1 teaspoon vinegar
1 4-ounce can sliced mushrooms, drained
1 Tablespoon minced parsley
½ cup grated Romano cheese

Combine flour, salt and pepper. Dredge chicken in flour mixture and brown in hot shortening. Drain chicken on paper towels. Pour off all but 1 Tablespoon of pan drippings.

Sauté onion in reserved drippings until tender. Add next 10 ingredients, stirring well. Return chicken to skillet; cover and simmer 45 minutes or until tender. At serving time, sprinkle chicken with ½ cup grated cheese. Serve over spaghetti and garnish with parsley sprigs, if desired.

Serves
4 to 6

CHICKEN ALFREDO

3 Tablespoons grated Parmesan cheese
2 eggs
1 Tablespoon water
3 whole chicken breasts, split, boned and skinned
½ to ¾ cup flour
1½ cups seasoned bread crumbs
½ cup butter
6 1-ounce slices mozzarella cheese
Parsley

Sauce
½ cup butter
1 pint whipping cream
3 Tablespoons grated Romano or Parmesan cheese

Beat together Parmesan cheese, eggs and water and set aside.

Flatten chicken breasts and dip in flour, egg mixture and then coat well in bread crumbs. Sauté slowly in butter until golden and done. Remove chicken to large, shallow baking dish. Place slice of cheese on each piece.

Meanwhile, heat butter, whipping cream and cheese until smooth. Pour sauce over chicken and sprinkle with parsley. This can be done early in the day. Cover with foil until ½ hour before meal. Remove foil and bake at 350° 20 to 30 minutes until bubbling.

Serves
4 to 6

CREAMED CHICKEN

Easy and different way to use leftovers.

½ cup butter
2 Tablespoons flour
2 cups milk
3 Tablespoons sweet pickle relish
Dash Tabasco Sauce
Salt and pepper to taste
2 cups cubed cooked chicken or turkey

Make white sauce with butter, flour and milk, stirring until thick. Add salt, pepper, pickle relish and tabasco. Add chicken. Simmer 10 to 15 minutes.

Serve over toast or English muffins.

Serves 4

MEXICAN CHICKEN

2 whole chicken breasts, cooked and cut in large chunks
1 cup sour cream
10 large black olives, sliced
1 scallion with top, chopped
1 4½-ounce can chopped green chiles
1 10¾-ounce can cream of chicken soup
1 cup grated longhorn or Cheddar cheese

Place chicken pieces in 8x8-inch baking dish. Mix remaining ingredients, except cheese, and pour over chicken. Sprinkle with cheese.

Bake, covered, 1 hour at 350°.

Serve in warm flour tortillas or over rice.

Serves 4

BAKED CHICKEN SUPREME

4 cups cooked cut-up chicken
4 cups thinly-sliced celery
1 cup chopped pecans
2 cups mayonnaise
4 Tablespoons onion, chopped fine
4 Tablespoons lemon juice
1 cup grated Tilamook cheese
2 cups crushed potato chips
¼ cup chopped pecans

Lightly toss chicken, celery and pecans. Puree mayonnaise, onion, lemon juice and cheese to make a sauce and fold in chicken mixture. Spread in casserole and top with potato chips and pecans. Bake at 450° for 10 to 15 minutes. Serve hot.

Serves 8

CHICKEN ENCHILADAS

1 cup chopped onion
2 cloves garlic, minced
1 Tablespoon vegetable oil
2 to 2½ cups cooked chicken or turkey, cubed
1 7-ounce can diced green chiles
Salt to taste
6 ounces tomato paste
1 cup grated Velveeta cheese
½ cup margarine
2 Tablespoons flour
2 10¾-ounce cans chicken broth
12 small corn tortillas
Swiss cheese

Sauté onions and garlic in oil until tender. Add chicken, green chiles, salt, tomato paste and Velveeta cheese. Simmer until cheese melts.

Make sauce of margarine, flour and chicken broth. Cook until thickened; cool slightly. Dip tortilla in broth mixture to soften. Fill tortilla down center with 2 Tablespoons chicken mixture. Roll and place seam down in 8″ x 12″ baking dish. Continue with remaining tortillas, placing close together. Place slice of Swiss cheese on top of each enchilada. Pour remaining broth mixture over enchiladas. Bake at 350° 30 to 45 minutes, or until bubbly.

Can be made a day ahead, refrigerated, and baked just before serving.

Serves 6 to 8

CHICKEN BROCCOLI CASSEROLE

2 10-ounce packages frozen broccoli spears
3 whole chicken breasts
2 10½-ounce cans cream of chicken soup
1 cup mayonnaise
1 Tablespoon lemon juice
½ teaspoon curry powder
½ cup shredded sharp cheese
1 Tablespoon melted butter
½ cup dry bread crumbs
½ cup toasted, buttered slivered almonds

Cook broccoli until crisp-tender. Bake seasoned chicken breasts until tender in slow (325°) oven, covered with foil.

Remove skin and bones and cut in large pieces.

Place broccoli in bottom of 8½″ x 11″ casserole; add chicken.

Combine soup, mayonnaise, lemon juice, curry powder, and pour over chicken. Sprinkle with cheese, crumbs, butter and almonds.

Bake at 350° for 15 minutes covered. Remove cover and cook additional 15 minutes.

Can easily be doubled.

Serves 6.

FASHION SHOW CHICKEN SOUFFLE

6 slices white bread
2 cups diced chicken
¼ pound mushrooms, sauteed in
  2 Tablespoons butter or margarine
4 ounces water chestnuts, drained and sliced
¼ cup mayonnaise
4 slices sharp cheese
1 cup milk
½ teaspoon salt
2 eggs, beaten
1 10½-ounce can cream of celery soup
1 2-ounce jar of pimiento
1 cup buttered bread crumbs

Line 9″ x 13″ pan with bread.

Top with chicken, mushrooms, and chestnuts. Dot with mayonnaise. Top with cheese.

Combine eggs, milk, soup, and salt. Pour over casserole. Cover with foil and refrigerate overnight.

Bake uncovered at 350° for 1 hour. Add bread crumbs last 15 minutes.

Serves 6

QUICK CURRY ENTREE

1 small apple, peeled and chopped
2 Tablespoons chopped onion
2 Tablespoons butter
2 teaspoons curry powder
3 cloves or 1/16 teaspoon powdered clove
1 teaspoon lemon juice
3 cups lamb or chicken gravy
2 to 3 cups cooked lamb or chicken

Brown apple and onion in butter. Make into a paste and add curry powder, cloves and lemon juice. Simmer slowly for 10 minutes. Add curry mixture to lamb or chicken gravy. Place cooked meat in gravy mixture and simmer for 10 minutes. Serve with rice.

Serves
4 to 6

STUFFED TROUT

6 trout
2 lemons

Stuffing
½ pound mushrooms, sliced
1 onion, minced
olive oil
2 cups sour cream
2 6½-ounce cans clams
2 4½-ounce cans shrimp
1 medium bell pepper, finely shredded
½ teaspoon allspice
½ teaspoon paprika
¼ teaspoon coarse ground pepper

Place each trout on an individual piece of oiled heavy-duty aluminum foil. Stuff each fish with some clam-shrimp mixture. Sprinkle with the juice of the lemons. Carefully wrap and seal each package. Bake at 325° for about 30 minutes.

For stuffing, sauté mushrooms and onion in olive oil. In a separate bowl, combine the sour cream, clams, shrimp, bell pepper and spices. Add the sauteed mushrooms and onions.

Serves 6

BAKED FISH OLE

6 slices white fish (sea bass, sole, etc.)
½ teaspoon salt
¼ teaspoon black pepper
¼ teaspoon cayenne
¼ teaspoon mace
1 Tablespoon olive or salad oil
1 large onion, thinly sliced
2 Tablespoons pimiento, diced
6 thick slices of tomato
3 Tablespoons snipped green onion tops
1 cup thinly sliced mushrooms
½ cup white wine
1 cup dry bread crumbs
½ cup butter, melted

Wipe fish with damp cloth. Sprinkle with seasonings.

Spread oil over bottom of 12 x 8 x 2-inch baking dish. Arrange onion slices and pimiento in bottom of dish. Top with seasoned fish slices, arranged side by side. Cover each piece of fish with a tomato slice; sprinkle with green onions. Scatter mushrooms over all; add wine. Brown crumbs in melted butter; sprinkle over top of fish. Bake, uncovered, at 350° 35 to 40 minutes or until fish is tender and flakes easily.

Serves
4 to 6

FILET OF SOLE STUFFED WITH LOBSTER

A seafood lover's delight!

½ pound small mushrooms, chopped
½ cup chopped onion
2 Tablespoons butter
½ cup lobster
1 cup soft white bread crumbs
3 Tablespoons Parmesan cheese
4 marinated artichoke hearts, chopped
½ to 1 teaspoon salt
½ teaspoon pepper
8 sole filets
2 cups white wine (Chablis)
Lemon wedges

Sauce
1 cup medium white sauce made with white wine or 1 package wine sauce mix
½ pound fresh tiny cocktail shrimp
¼ pound mushroom caps, sliced
½ cup liquid from sole casserole

In a saucepan, sauté mushrooms and onions in butter. Remove from heat and add lobster. Mix together bread crumbs, cheese, artichoke hearts, salt and pepper and place equal amounts of filling on each filet. Roll filets and secure with a toothpick. Place the rolls in a glass dish and cover with white wine. Marinate for 4 hours or overnight.

Transfer rolls and marinade to shallow casserole and bake at 350° for 40 minutes.

Remove fish from casserole and keep hot. Discard all but ½ cup of the broth to be used in preparing the sauce.

Sauce: In a small pan, prepare white sauce. Stir in shrimp, mushrooms and reserved broth, blending thoroughly.

Pour sauce over sole and serve with lemon wedges.

Serves 8

GEORGE'S BARBECUED SALMON

5 to 7 pound salmon

Mama Phoebe's Barbecue Sauce
½ cup butter
1 cup catsup
4 Tablespoons soy sauce
2 Tablespoons prepared mustard
1 Tablespoon lemon juice
Dash of pepper and Worcestershire sauce

Filet fish.

To make sauce, combine all ingredients and simmer 15 minutes.

Grill fish, skin side down, over hot coals, 10 to 15 minutes, depending on size of fish, or until meat is white from sides to halfway up, brushing generously with sauce every 3 or 4 minutes.

Divide into 3-inch or 4-inch steaks with edge of spatula, and turn each over on skin, which remains on the grill. Baste and barbecue 10 to 12 minutes more.

Serve with sauce.

BARBECUED STUFFED FISH

A great patio entree.

8- to 10-pound whole fish
Salt and pepper
½ cup melted butter
¼ cup lemon juice

Garden Vegetable Stuffing
½ cup finely chopped onion
¼ cup butter
2 cups dry bread cubes
1 cup coarsely shredded carrots
1 cup sliced mushrooms
½ cup snipped parsley
¼ cup chopped green pepper
1½ Tablespoon lemon juice
1 egg
1 clove garlic, minced
1 teaspoon salt
¼ teaspoon marjoram leaves
¼ teaspoon lemon pepper

Wash fish quickly in cold water and pat dry. Rub cavity with salt and pepper.

Prepare stuffing. Sauté onion in butter until tender. Lightly mix in remaining ingredients. Stuff fish; close opening with skewers and lace with string. Brush fish with salad oil.

Put fish in wire basket or wrap in foil and grill 4 to 6 inches from medium hot coals for 45 minutes or until fish flakes easily with fork, turning 3 times and basting with mixture of butter and lemon juice.

Serves 10.

BAKED FISH WITH WINE SAUCE

4 pounds fish fillets (red snapper or sole)
3 Tablespoons butter
2 Tablespoons chopped carrots
2 Tablespoons minced onions
1 Tablespoon flour
1 cup white wine
1 cup cream
Salt and pepper to taste

Melt butter in heavy pan; cook carrots and onions until soft but not brown. Stir in flour and gradually add wine and cream. Simmer until thickened. Season to taste with salt and pepper.

Place fish in shallow baking dish and pour sauce over. Bake in 375° oven for 30 minutes, basting frequently.

Serves 6 to 8

CHEEZY SWORDFISH

¾ cup milk
1½ pounds swordfish steak
¼ teaspoon salt
¼ teaspoon pepper
2 Tablespoons butter
¼ cup Chablis wine
2 Tablespoons lemon juice
Chopped spinach or chopped broccoli (optional)

Zesty Cheese Sauce
2 Tablespoons butter
2 Tablespoons flour
½ cup milk (from marinade)
¼ cup heavy cream
½ cup Chablis wine
⅔ cup grated sharp Cheddar cheese
1 teaspoon Worcestershire sauce
Salt and pepper to taste

Pour the milk into a shallow dish. Lay the swordfish steak in the milk and cover the dish. Refrigerate the fish for ½ hour, turning once. Remove the fish from the milk and reserve ½ cup of the milk for the sauce. Season the fish with salt and pepper. Melt the butter in a baking dish. Lay the fish in the butter and turn it to coat both sides. Pour the wine and lemon juice over the fish. Bake, uncovered, at 350° for 15 minutes. Pour the sauce over the swordfish and bake for another 5 minutes or until the fish flakes easily.

Sauce: On low heat, melt the butter in a saucepan and slowly blend in the flour. Add the milk and cream a little at a time, stirring constantly. Add the wine and continue stirring. Add the cheese and stir until it is completely melted. Remove the saucepan from the heat, stir in the Worcestershire sauce, salt and pepper.

Serves 4

FATHER CARL'S SCALLOPS

1 pound scallops
12 ounces fresh mushrooms
4 ounces shallots, chopped
3 cups Chablis
2 Tablespoons flour
2 Tablespoons butter
Salt and pepper to taste
2 cups light cream
8 ounces Swiss cheese, grated

Cook scallops with mushrooms, shallots and Chablis. Boil for 2 minutes; remove scallops and vegetables and reduce liquid to one cup. Thicken with flour and butter to make very thick. If necessary, add additional equal parts of flour and butter to make wine liquid very thick. Then add light cream to make desired thickness. Pour over scallops and vegetables and mix. Fill scallop shells, top with cheese and bake until brown.

Bake 350°
15 minutes

Makes 8 appetizers
or 4 entrees

SHRIMP SCAMPI

¾ pound medium size shrimp
6 Tablespoons margarine or butter
1 Tablespoon sliced green onions
1 Tablespoon olive oil or salad oil
4 or 5 cloves of garlic, minced or pressed, or
½ teaspoon garlic powder
2 teaspoons lemon juice
2 Tablespoons chopped parsley
¼ teaspoon grated lemon peel
Tabasco sauce

Shell and devein shrimp. Butterfly, if large enough.

Melt butter in frying pan over medium heat. Add onion, oil, garlic, lemon juice and pinch of salt. Cook about 2 or 3 minutes, until bubbly. Add shrimp and cook about 5 minutes, til they turn pink, stirring and turning as necessary. Blend in parsley, grated lemon peel and dash or two of tabasco sauce.

Serve immediately with lemon wedges or tartar sauce.

Serves 2

KING CRAB AU GRATIN

4 6-ounce packages frozen king or snow crab
2 Tablespoons butter or margarine
3 Tablespoons flour
1 cup milk
½ cup light cream
½ cup chicken broth
¾ cup shredded sharp Cheddar cheese
1 4-ounce can sliced mushrooms, drained
2 Tablespoons grated onion
1 teaspoon salt
¼ teaspoon paprika
2 Tablespoons white wine (optional)
¼ cup fine dry bread crumbs

Defrost crab. Drain.

Melt butter or margarine in saucepan. Stir in flour until smooth. Gradually stir in milk, cream and chicken broth. Cook, stirring constantly, over low heat until sauce is smooth and thick. Add cheese, mushrooms, onion, salt, paprika and wine. Stir until cheese is melted. Stir in chunks of crab. Pour mixture into a well greased 1½ quart casserole. Sprinkle bread crumbs over top. Bake at 400° 10 to 15 minutes or until top is golden brown. Serve over hot cooked rice.

Serves 6

SIZZLING QUAIL

There is something exotic about a flaming entree. This is a simple recipe to follow. The flambé adds the enchantment.

- 10 quail, cleaned and skinned
- Salt and pepper
- ¾ cup butter
- 1 teaspoon dry basil
- ½ cup plus 3 Tablespoons good brandy
- 4½-ounce can chopped black olives
- ¼ cup shallots

Sprinkle the quail with salt and pepper.

Melt the butter in a large skillet over low heat. Stir in the basil. Add the birds and sauté, stirring constantly, for about 5 minutes. Add ½ cup brandy, olives and shallots and stir thoroughly. Cover and reduce heat. Simmer for 20 to 25 minutes, basting frequently. If more liquid is necessary, add a little brandy.

To flame, bring the quail to the table in the pan. Uncover and add 3 Tablespoons of brandy to the pan. Flame with a long taper.

Serves
5 to 7

LIQUEUR QUAIL

8 or 10 quail, cleaned and skinned
1½ cups Cassis (black-currant liqueur)
1/3 cup cooking oil
Salt and pepper

Cassis Sauce
1 cup water
½ cup seedless white raisins
1 cup reserved marinade
½ cup Cassis liquer
1 Tablespoon black cherry jam
1 cup chicken broth or bouillon
3 Tablespoons flour

Combine Cassis, oil, salt and pepper and pour over quail in shallow pan. Marinate the quail covered and refrigerated for 4 hours, turning the birds once. After the quail are marinated, remove them from the pan; reserve 1 cup of the marinade for the sauce. Arrange the quail in a single layer, breast up, in a baking dish. Pour the sauce on top. Cover and bake at 350° for 30 minutes.

Cassis Sauce: Boil 1 cup of water and pour it over the raisins; cover and let them steep for 5 minutes. In the meantime, combine the 1 cup of reserved marinade, liqueur, jam and chicken broth. Heat slowly at low temperature; gradually add flour to thicken the sauce, stirring constantly. Drain the raisins and add them to the sauce.

Serves
4 or 5

QUAIL IN A PAN

10 quail, cleaned
4 Tablespoons butter
1 cup shredded carrots
½ cup sliced green onions
¼ cup fresh snipped parsley
1 cup raw long grain rice
3 cups chicken broth
½ teaspoon salt
Dash of pepper
2 slices bacon, cut up

Brown the whole birds in butter, then remove and set aside.

In the same skillet, cook the carrots, onions and parsley until tender, stirring often. Add the rice and mix thoroughly. Add the chicken broth, salt and pepper. Place the birds on top of the mixture. Sprinkle with additional salt and pepper. Place some bacon on top of each bird. Cover and cook for 30 minutes, or until tender.

Remove the bacon and serve.

Serves 5 or 6

QUAIL PAPRIKA

6 quail, cleaned
1 teaspoon salt
¼ teaspoon pepper
3 Tablespoons flour
½ cup butter
¾ cup sour cream

Sauce
2 10¾-ounce cans cream of mushroom soup
1 cup water
3 Tablespoons paprika

Rub the quail inside and out with salt and pepper. Tie the legs close to the body. Sprinkle with 2 Tablespoons of flour. Brown the quail in butter for 6 minutes. Place the birds in a casserole

For sauce, combine soup, water and paprika in a mixing bowl and stir until well blended.

Pour sauce over. Bake, covered in a 350° oven for 25 minutes or until tender. Remove the quail to a warm platter, leaving juices in pan. Stir the remaining flour into the pan juices. Add the sour cream; mix and heat but do not allow the sauce to come to a boil. Season to taste. Pour over the quail.

Serves 4 to 6

ROAST GOOSE AND FRUIT

1 wild goose, 5 to 6 pounds, cleaned
1 lemon, cut into quarters
Salt and pepper
¼ cup melted bacon fat
4 thick slices bacon

Fruit and Nut Stuffing
3 Golden Delicious apples
2 Tablespoons lemon juice
1 cup white raisins, steeped in hot water
1 cup chopped walnuts
1 cup cooked wild rice
1 teaspoon cinnamon
¼ teaspoon nutmeg
¼ cup brown sugar, firmly packed
¼ cup vermouth

Basting Liquid
½ cup apple jelly
⅔ cup dry vermouth
½ teaspoon nutmeg
Pan drippings

Rub goose inside and out with the cut lemon and sprinkle with salt and pepper. To prepare stuffing, core and pare the apples, cut them into chunks and sprinkle with lemon juice. Combine with the remaining ingredients. Spoon the stuffing loosely into the goose cavity and skewer closed. Cover the goose with cheesecloth soaked in melted bacon fat, then place bacon strips over cheesecloth. Put goose, breast up, on a rack in a roasting pan. To prepare basting liquid, heat the ingredients in a saucepan over low heat, stirring until the jelly liquefies. Add the pan drippings and stir. Roast at 325°, basting frequently. Roast the bird for approximately 25 minutes per pound until done. If the age of the bird is unknown, tenderize it by pouring 1 cup water into the roasting pan and keeping it covered during the last hour of roasting. Remove pan drippings and save.

STUFFED CORNISH GAME HEN

4 Cornish game hens

Stuffing
1 cup wild rice
¾ cup raisins
½ cup blanched almonds
1 6-ounce can water chestnuts, sliced

Baste
½ cup butter
1 cup orange juice

Sauce
1 cup pineapple-apricot jam
⅔ cup dry vermouth
⅔ cup sliced spricots, canned or fresh
¼ cup butter, melted

Stuff the Cornish game hens and bake at 350° 1¼ hours. Baste birds throughout cooking time. Slice birds lengthwise and serve with sauce.

To make stuffing, cook rice as directed. When cooked, add raisins, almonds and water chestnuts and mix well.

To make baste, combine butter and orange juice until blended.

To make sauce, combine all ingredients and heat.

VINO, GRAPES AND DOVE

12 doves, cleaned
2 red onions, sliced ¼ inch thick
2 cups seedless grapes
Salt and pepper
3 Tablespoons butter
½ cup melted butter
½ cup dry white wine
1 cup chicken broth

Stuff each dove with onion slices and a few grapes. Close the openings with fine skewers and season the outside with salt and pepper. Brown the birds in the 3 Tablespoons of butter. Brush the outside of the birds with the baste. Place the birds in a baking dish and roast in a 350° oven for 45 minutes, basting frequently.

Combine the melted butter, wine and broth to make a basting liquid.

Serves 4 to 6

HUNTER'S HARE

2 rabbits, cut up

Marinade
½ cup white wine or dry sherry
¼ cup red wine (preferably Burgundy)
½ cup olive oil
1 teaspoon each of tarragon, Beau Monde and salt
1 clove garlic, minced
3 Tablespoons chopped fresh parsley
½ teaspoon chopped chives
Dash of pepper

Combine ingredients for marinade and marinate the rabbit for two hours or longer. Barbecue the rabbit on a greased grill over very hot coals for approximately 45 minutes. While barbecuing, baste with the reserved marinade.

Serves 4 to 6.

vegetables

ITALIAN GREEN BEANS

Thirty calories per serving!!

1 10-ounce package frozen Italian green beans
2 tomatoes, diced
½ cup diced green pepper
1 Tablespoon finely chopped green onions
⅛ teaspoon rosemary leaves
⅛ teaspoon basil
⅛ teaspoon oregano

Cook beans as directed on package. Drain, reserving ¼ cup liquid. Place reserved liquid and rest of ingredients in sauce pan. Cook, uncovered, over low heat until green pepper is tender, about 20 minutes. Stir in beans and cook 5 minutes more.

Serves 4.

GREEN BEANS WITH MUSTARD SAUCE

2 pounds frozen green beans
½ cup olive oil
1 Tablespoon Dijon mustard
Juice of 1 lemon
Salt and pepper to taste

Cook beans as directed on package and drain.

Prepare sauce by adding oil to other ingredients.

Toss beans with sauce one or two hours before serving.

Reheat and serve warm.

Serves 6 to 8

BROCCOLI CASSEROLE

2 10½-ounce packages frozen chopped broccoli
2 eggs, beaten
1 cup mayonnaise
1 10½-ounce can celery soup
½ cup milk
1 cup grated sharp Cheddar cheese
1 Tablespoon onion flakes
1 teaspoon Worcestershire sauce
Salt and pepper to taste
⅓ cup cracker crumbs
Butter

Partially cook broccoli. Drain and cool.

Mix remaining ingredients, combine with broccoli and pour into large buttered casserole. Top with cracker crumbs and butter and bake at 350° for 45 minutes.

Serves 6 to 8

CARROTS WINEMASTER

- 2 pounds carrots
- 3 stalks celery with leaves, diced
- ½ large onion, diced
- ¾ cup white wine
- ⅓ cup sugar
- ¼ cup butter
- ½ teaspoon dill weed

Scrape carrots and cut into ¼-inch slices.

Combine all ingredients in saucepan and cook over low heat until tender.

Serves 8

BACON-FRIED CARROTS

The bacon gives carrots a new taste.

- 3 slices bacon
- 1 pound carrots, sliced
- 1 medium onion, chopped
- ½ teaspoon salt
- ⅛ teaspoon pepper

Cook bacon slices until crisp. Remove from skillet, saving drippings, crumble and set aside.

Cook remaining ingredients slowly in bacon drippings, covered, about 10 minutes or until slightly tender. Uncover and cook until carrots are slightly browned, stirring occasionally. Add bacon and serve.

Serves 4

COMPANY CARROTS

Two bunches young carrots or two 1-pound cans fingerling carrots
½ cup mayonnaise
1 Tablespoon minced onion (fresh or instant)
1 Tablespoon prepared horseradish
Salt and pepper to taste
½ cup fine cracker crumbs
Paprika or minced parsley

Cook whole carrots until just tender, reserving ½ cup cooking water. Arrange carrots in buttered, flat baking dish.

Combine mayonnaise, onion, horseradish, salt, pepper and cooking water. Pour sauce over carrots, dot with butter, sprinkle with cracker crumbs and bake, uncovered at 375° 15 to 20 minutes. Garnish with paprika or parsley to serve.

Serves 6

CHEESE CAULIFLOWER WITH ALMOND TOPPING

1 large head cauliflower
4 ounces packaged herb stuffing mix
⅓ cup slivered, toasted almonds
2 teaspoons chicken stock base
1 cup milk
3 ounces Swiss Gruyere cheese
1 teaspoon Dijon-style mustard
½ cup water
¼ cup butter
½ of an 8-ounce package of herb stuffing mix
⅓ cup slivered, toasted almonds

Trim whole cauliflower and cook, covered, in boiling salted water until just tender, about 25 minutes. Drain and gently separate into flowerets. Place in 2-quart greased casserole.

In a saucepan, melt ¼ cup butter and stir in the flour and chicken stock base to make a smooth paste. Gradually add milk; cook, stirring until thickened. Add cheese and mustard and continue cooking until blended and smooth. Pour sauce over cauliflower.

Heat together the water and remaining ¼ cup butter. Pour in stuffing mix, add nuts and combine thoroughly. Spread over cauliflower and bake, uncoverd in 400° oven for 20 minutes.

For alternate recipe: Double the recipe for sauce and topping. Cook 2 8-ounce packages frozen broccoli spears til barely tender. Put cooked cauliflower in one half of a 9 x 13-inch baking dish and broccoli in the other half; pour sauce over and cover with topping.

Serves 8

BAKED SWISS CAULIFLOWER

1 large head cauliflower
½ cup bread crumbs
2 cups shredded Swiss cheese
1½ cups half and half
3 egg yolks, beaten
½ teaspoon salt
¼ teaspoon pepper
¼ teaspoon nutmeg
¼ cup melted butter

Wash cauliflower and break into flowerets. Cook covered in salted water for 15 minutes.

Placed drained cauliflower in buttered 1½-quart shallow casserole. Combine remaining ingredients, except butter, and add to cauliflower. Pour butter over top and bake in 350° oven for 20 minutes.

Serves 6 to 8

FRENCH ONION CASSEROLE

This one-dish casserole is done completely in your microwave oven.

4 medium onions, thinly sliced
3 Tablespoons butter or margarine
2 Tablespoons all-purpose flour
Dash of pepper
¾ cup beef bouillon
¼ cup dry sherry
½ cup plain croutons
2 Tablespoons butter or margarine, melted
½ cup shredded Swiss cheese
3 Tablespoons grated Parmesan cheese
Paprika

Place onions and butter in a 1½ quart casserole. Micro-cook, covered, 7 minutes on High or until onion is tender; stir once or twice. Blend in flour and pepper. Add bouillon and sherry. Micro-cook 2½ to 3 minutes or until thickened on High; stir 2 or 3 times during cooking.

Toss croutons with butter. Spoon over onion mixture. Sprinkle with cheeses, then paprika. Micro-cook 3 minutes, on Medium, or until cheese is melted.

Serves 4 to 6

GOURMET ONIONS

Quick and easy, yet elegant.

- 10 to 12 boiling onions, peeled, cooked and drained
- 3 Tablespoons butter
- ½ teaspoon monosodium glutamate
- ½ teaspoon sugar
- ¼ teaspoon salt
- ¼ teaspoon pepper
- ¼ cup sherry
- ¼ cup shredded Parmesan cheese

Cook onions in boiling water 5 minutes. Drain.

Melt butter in saucepan and stir in spices and sherry. Add onions and heat quickly, about 5 minutes, stirring occasionally. Turn into serving dish and sprinkle with cheese.

Serves 6

MAME'S MEXICAN PEPPERS

3 large bell peppers
1 pound ricotta cheese
1 egg
Salt and pepper to taste
¾ pound chili pepper cheese, grated
1 7-ounce can taco sauce

Cut each bell pepper into quarters or halves and hollow out. Par boil for 7 to 9 minutes (they should maintain some firmness).

In a bowl, mix the ricotta cheese, egg, salt and pepper and three-fourths of the chili pepper cheese. Stuff each bell pepper section with cheese mixture. Sprinkle with remaining grated cheese. Arrange in pan.

Spoon taco sauce over each bell pepper section. Bake in 325° over for ½ hour.

Serves
4 to 6

POTATOES MAXINE

1 32-ounce package shredded (hash brown) frozen potatoes
1 10½-ounce can cream of chicken soup plus ½ can milk
2 cups sour cream
2 cups shredded Cheddar cheese
½ cup grated onion
½ cup melted butter
Salt and pepper to taste

Topping
2 cups crumbled corn flakes (not boxed corn flake crumbs)
¼ cup butter, melted

Combine ingredients in 8″ x 12″ glass dish and sprinkle with topping. Bake at 350° 45 minutes.

For topping, combine corn flake crumbs and butter.

Serves 8 to 12

POTATOES ROMANOFF

5 cups diced, cooked potatoes
1 clove garlic, minced
1½ teaspoons salt
¼ cup chopped onion
1 cup sour cream
2 cups creamed cottage cheese
1 10-ounce package frozen chopped spinach, cooked and drained
¾ cup shredded Cheddar cheese

Sprinkle salt over potatoes and garlic. Fold together onion, sour cream, cottage cheese, and spinach. Mix well with potatoes, and put all in a buttered 2½-quart casserole. Sprinkle with cheese.

Bake at 350° for 45 minutes.

Serves 8

CRAB-STUFFED POTATOES

4 medium Idaho potatoes
½ cup butter
½ cup light cream
1 teaspoon salt
Dash of pepper
4 teaspoons grated onion
1 cup grated sharp Cheddar cheese
1 6½-ounce can crabmeat
Paprika

Scrub potatoes well and dry. Bake at 375° until soft, about 1 hour.

Cut potatoes in half lengthwise, scoop out, and whip. Add butter, cream, salt, pepper, onion and cheese, and mix well. With a fork, mix in crabmeat and refill shells. Sprinkle with paprika and reheat in 450° oven for 15 minutes.

Can be made a day ahead and refrigerated, or frozen.

Serves 4 to 8.

SPINACH TOMATO CUPS

3 slices bacon
¼ cup chopped onion
8 ounces chopped fresh spinach
½ cup sour cream
Dash of hot pepper sauce
4 medium tomatoes
½ cup shredded mozzarella cheese

Cook bacon til crisp. Drain, saving 2 Tablespoons of bacon drippings. Crumble bacon.

Cook onion in drippings 'til tender. Stir in spinach. Cook approximately 5 minutes til tender. Remove from heat and add sour cream, bacon and hot sauce.

Cut tops from tomatoes. Hollow and drain. Fill tomatoes with spinach mixture. Place in 8 x 8 x 2-inch pan. Bake 25 minutes at 375°. Top with cheese and bake an additional 2 or 3 minutes.

Serves 4

STUFFED PATTY PAN SQUASH

2 pounds patty pan squash (each about 3 inches wide)
Boiling, salted water
Salt and pepper
3 Tablespoons butter or margarine
6 green onions (with part of green tops), thinly sliced
1 4-ounce can chopped green chiles, drained
2 Tablespoons flour
½ cup chicken broth or milk
¼ teaspoon poultry seasoning
½ cup grated Parmesan cheese
½ cup soft, fresh bread crumbs

Cook whole squash in the boiling salted water until just tender, about 5 minutes; drain. Cut off stems, then cut a ½ inch thick slice off blossom end of each squash; chop slices and set aside. Remove all seeds, arrange squash in a baking dish and sprinkle with salt and pepper.

Melt 2 Tablespoons of the butter, add onions, chiles and flour and cook until bubbly. Stir in the broth and cook, stirring, until thickened. Remove from heat and add chopped squash, poultry seasoning, and cheese; fill each squash. Then melt the remaining 1 Tablespoon butter, mix with crumbs and sprinkle over squash. Bake, uncovered, in 350° oven for 20 to 30 minutes, until lightly browned.

Serves 8

SUPER SQUASH

1 small butternut squash, cut up
4 or 5 zucchini, cut up
2 or 3 tomatoes, cut up
¼ cup butter, cut in small pieces
¼ onion, cut in rings
2 teaspoons sugar
1 teaspoon salt
½ teaspoon pepper
¼ teaspoon oregano or Italian seasoning
Parmesan cheese

Mix everything but cheese in casserole. Cover and bake 45 minutes at 350°.

Sprinkle with Parmesan cheese and bake 15 minutes more.

Serves 6 to 8

TOMATOES LUTECE

8 firm, ripe tomatoes, peeled
¼ cup chopped parsley
1 clove garlic, crushed
1 teaspoon salt
1 teaspoon sugar
¼ teaspoon pepper
¼ cup salad oil
2 Tablespoons tarragon vinegar
2 teaspoons prepared mustard

Cut out stems from peeled tomatoes; slice crosswise into ½-inch slices and reform into tomato shape.

Combine remaining ingredients in small jar, cover, shake well and pour over tomatoes.

Let stand at room temperature 20 minutes before serving.

Serves 8

ZUCCHINI SOUFLE

2 cups grated zucchini
4 Tablespoons butter
2 Tablespoons chopped shallots
Pepper to taste
1 cup milk
3 Tablespoons butter
3 Tablespoons flour
3 egg yolks
1 cup Parmesan cheese
5 egg whites

Layer grated zucchini with salt. Let stand 30 minutes.

Melt 3 Tablespoons butter in saucepan. Add flour. Cook 2 minutes. Add milk and cook, stirring constantly, until thick. Whisk in egg yolks. Sauté shallots in 4 Tablespoons butter. Drain and squeeze zucchini. Add zucchini to shallots and barely heat. Add zucchini and Parmesan to sauce. Beat egg whites until stiff. Fold the mixtures together. Coat souffle dish with butter and sprinkle with Parmesan. Pour mixture in dish. Souffle may sit one hour, covered, before baking.

Bake at 350° for 35 minutes.

QUICK DELUXE CASSEROLE

1 10½-ounce package frozen cauliflower
or 1 small head fresh cauliflower
1 10½-ounce package frozen peas
6 medium carrots, sliced thick and cooked
Salt to taste
1½ cups white sauce
⅓ pound Colby cheese, grated
½ cup butter
½ cup cracker crumbs

White Sauce
1 Tablespoon butter or margarine
1 Tablespoon flour
¼ teaspoon salt
Dash of white pepper
1½ cups milk

Thaw frozen cauliflower enough to break apart. If using fresh cauliflower, steam for a few minutes, then break apart. Place vegetables in casserole dish. Salt to taste.

Make white sauce by melting butter or margarine in saucepan over low heat. Blend in flour, salt and dash of white pepper. Add milk all at once. Cook quickly, stirring constantly, til mixture thickens and bubbles.

Add cheese to sauce to melt and pour sauce over vegetables.

For topping, melt butter and pour over cracker crumbs. Sprinkle crumbs on top of vegetables and bake in preheated 350° oven for 20 minutes.

Serves 6

VEGETABLE BURRITOS

¼ cup oil
2 garlic cloves, minced
1 large onion, chopped
1 6-ounce can water chestnuts, drained and sliced
2 large zucchini, grated
½ pound mushrooms, sliced
2 large tomatoes
Salt and pepper
1 teaspoons celery salt
8 8-inch flour tortillas
2 cups shredded Cheddar cheese
1 cup fresh guacamole, or
1 6-ounce can frozen avocado dip
1 pint sour cream

Heat oil in large skillet over high heat. Add garlic and onion; sauté til golden. Add water chestnuts, stir until warm. Add zucchini and heat through. Add mushrooms, stir until tender. Add tomatoes and heat through. Sprinkle with salt, pepper and celery salt. Remove from heat — do not overcoook.

Fill each tortilla down middle with 2 Tablespoons grated cheese and 2 Tablespoons vegetable filling using slotted spoon. Roll tortilla and place seam side down in 9x12-inch baking dish.

Can be prepared up to this point 2 or 3 hours ahead of serving. Cover while standing, do not refrigerate.

Heat at 350° 10 to 15 minutes.

Remove from oven and garnish with a row of guacamole and a row of sour cream.

Serves 8

cookies

PEANUT BUTTER COOKIES

1 cup peanut butter
½ cup butter
1 cup honey
½ Tablespoon vanilla
2 cups whole wheat flour
½ teaspoons baking powder

Preheat over to 375°.

Cream the first four ingredients; add flour and baking powder and mix. Drop walnut sized balls on a greased cookie sheet. Flatten with a fork and bake 15 minutes.

Makes
3 to 4 dozen

PECAN SLICES

1 cup plus 2 Tablespoons flour
½ cup butter or margarine, softened
2 eggs
1½ cups brown sugar, firmly packed
1 cup chopped pecans
½ cup flaked coconut
½ teaspoon baking powder
½ teaspoon salt
1 teaspoon vanilla

Icing
1½ cups confectioners' sugar
Lemon juice

Preheat oven to 350°.

Combine 1 cup flour with butter and work with spoon until well blended. Spread in a 9 x 13-inch pan and bake for 12 minutes.

Beat the eggs and gradually add brown sugar, nuts and coconut, beating well. Add 2 Tablespoons flour which has been mixed with baking powder and salt. Add vanilla. Spread over dough and bake for 25 minutes.

For icing, mix lemon juice with sugar to spreading consistency and spread over cake when cool. Cut into 1 x 2-inch pieces.

Makes 4 dozen

PEANUT BUTTER PUFFS

1 egg white
Dash of salt
6 Tablespoons granulated sugar
¼ cup peanut butter

Preheat oven to 325°.

Beat egg white with salt until soft peaks form. Gradually add sugar, beating until stiff peaks form. Stir in peanut butter. Drop from teaspoon 1″ apart on greased cookie sheet. Bake 18 minutes or until lightly browned. Cool slightly before removing from pan to cooling rack.

Makes 1 dozen

RAISIN VANILLA DROP COOKIES

1½ cups raisins
1½ cups water
3½ cups flour
1 teaspoon baking soda
1 teaspoon salt
1 teaspoon baking powder
1 cup butter or margarine
1½ cups sugar
3 eggs
1 teaspoon vanilla

Simmer raisins in water until all liquid is absorbed. Cool at least 30 minutes.

Sift together dry ingredients.

Cream butter and sugar. Beat in eggs, one at a time. Blend in raisins and vanilla. Fold in flour mixture until dough is smooth and leaves sides of bowl. Drop by teaspoon into a small dish of sugar, roll into small balls and place on greased cookie sheet. Bake in preheated 350° oven for 12 minutes.

Makes 5 dozen.

BENNE SEED WAFERS

A pleasant, transparent-like wafer.

- ¾ cup benne (sesame) seeds
- ¼ pound butter (not margarine)
- 2 cups brown sugar
- 1 egg, beaten
- 1 cup all-purpose flour
- ½ teaspoon baking powder
- ¼ teaspoon salt
- 1 teaspoon vanilla

Spread the benne seeds on a cookie sheet and toast for 3 or 4 minutes at 375° and set aside. Line cookie sheets with aluminum foil. Cream butter and brown sugar, then add beaten eggs, flour, baking powder and salt. Mix well. Add benne seeds and vanilla. Drop by ½ teaspoonfuls onto ungreased, foil-lined pans. Bake at 375° for approximately 7 to 8 minutes. Allow to cool one minute before removing from pan.

Makes 100 wafers

ROLLED BUTTER COOKIES

These make a delicious cut-out cookie to decorate for a holiday.

3 cups flour
1 teaspoon baking soda
2 teaspoons cream of tartar
1 cup butter, softened
2 eggs
1 cup sugar
1 teaspoon vanilla
½ teaspoon almond extract

Sift dry ingredients together; work in butter. Add remaining ingredients, blending thoroughly. Chill dough for 20 minutes.

Roll dough on floured cloth and cut with cookie cutter. Bake in preheated 375° oven 8 to 10 minutes.

Makes 5 dozen

CRACKLED TOP MOLASSES COOKIES

1 cup granulated sugar
¾ cup shortening
1 egg, beaten
2 cups flour
¾ teaspoon salt
1 teaspoon cinnamon
1 teaspoon ginger
2 teaspoons baking soda
4 Tablespoons molasses

Preheat oven to 350°.

Cream sugar and shortening in large bowl until fluffy. Blend in egg.

Sift flour with salt, cinnamon and ginger.

Stir soda into molasses, adding alternately with dry mixture to creamed dough. When well blended, roll into small balls, flattening slightly with palm. Press one side in granulated sugar. Bake sugar side up for 10 minutes.

Makes 3 to 4
dozen

GRANTHAM GINGERBREAD BISCUITS

1½ cups self-rising flour
1 cup finely granulated sugar
½ teaspoon baking powder
1 heaping teaspoon ginger
1 egg
½ cup very soft butter or margarine

Preheat oven to 350°.

Mix dry ingredients.

Add egg to butter. Beat well and add to other ingredients. Mix well by hand. Make small balls of mixture. Place well apart on floured cookie sheet, pressing top slightly, and bake for 30 minutes. Do not allow to brown. Cookies will spread during baking.

YUMMY COOKIES

1 pound butter, softened
1 cup granulated sugar
3½ cups sifted flour
2 teaspoons vanilla
2 cups crushed potato chips

Preheat oven to 350°.

Cream butter and sugar. Stir in remaining ingredients. Roll dough in small balls, press flat with fork and bake on ungreased cookie sheet for 12 minutes.

Store in airtight container.

Makes 4 dozen.

RAISIN CRISPS

½ cup raisins
½ cup water
½ cup shortening
¾ cup granulated sugar
1¼ cups flour
½ teaspoon baking soda
¼ teaspoon salt
½ teaspoon cinnamon
½ teaspoon nutmeg
¼ teaspoon cloves

Preheat oven to 375°.

Cover raisins with water and bring to a boil. Drain and reserve ¼ cup water.

Cream shortening and sugar until light and fluffy.

Sift all remaining ingredients and add to creamed mixture with raisin water. Mix well. Add raisins. Drop by teaspoonful onto ungreased cookie sheet. Bake 10 to 12 minutes.

Makes 3 to 4 dozen

HONEYMOON BARS

These bars will keep up to a month in an air-tight container.

1⅓ cups unsifted all-purpose flour
½ teaspoon salt
½ cup butter, softened
½ cup firmly packed brown sugar or ¼ cup each granulated sugar and dark brown sugar

Topping
2 eggs
1 cup firmly packed light or dark brown sugar
1½ cups flaked coconut or 1½ cups chopped walnuts

Mix flour, salt, butter and brown sugar and press into a 9 x 9-inch greased pan. Bake at 350°*1 for 10 minutes. Remove from oven.*

For topping, beat eggs until fluffy, add brown sugar and coconut or nuts and mix well. Spread on partly baked pastry. Return to oven and bake at 350° 15 minutes. Cut in squares while hot.

Makes 3 dozen

BUTTER CREAM CHEESE BARS

1 18½-ounce golden butter recipe cake mix
2 eggs, slightly beaten
½ cup butter
2 eggs
8 ounces cream cheese, softened
1 pound box powdered sugar

Preheat oven to 350°.

Blend cake mix, two eggs and butter until pasty and spread in bottom of an ungreased 9 x 13-inch pan.

Beat eggs, cream cheese and sugar and spoon over cake mixture. Bake for 30 to 40 minutes. Cool, refrigerate and cut into bars. Freezes well.

CHOCOLATE MINT BROWNIES

4 ounces unsweetened chocolate
1 cup margarine
4 eggs
2 cups granulated sugar
1 cup flour
1 cup chopped nuts

Mint Frosting
3 cups confectioners' sugar
6 Tablespoons butter, softened
1 to 3 Tablespoons cream
2 Tablespoons peppermint extract
¼ teaspoon vanilla
¼ teaspoon green food coloring

Chocolate Frosting
3 ounces unsweetened chocolate
2 Tablespoons butter

Melt 4 ounces of chocolate and margarine; cool.

Beat eggs, sugar and flour. Stir in nuts and chocolate mixture. Spread in greased 10″ x 14″ pan. Bake at 350° for 15 minutes on lowest rack, 5 minutes more on highest rack. Remove and cool.

For mint frosting, beat all ingredients until smooth. Spread over brownies and refrigerate until well chilled.

For chocolate frosting, melt the chocolate with the butter and brush over the frosted brownies. Chill briefly. Cut into squares before glaze is too cold to prevent cracks on top layer.

These freeze well.

Makes 2 dozen

GINGER SNAPS

¾ cup shortening
1 cup sugar
¼ teaspoon salt
1 egg, beaten
4 Tablespoons molasses
2 cups all-purpose flour
2½ teaspoons baking soda
1 teaspoon ginger
1 teaspoon cinnamon
½ teaspoon cloves

Preheat oven to 300°.

Cream shortening and sugar. Blend in salt, beaten egg and molasses. Add dry ingredients to creamed mixture. Roll dough in small balls, the size of a walnut, and dip each ball in sugar. Flatten with fork which has been dipped in sugar. Bake 10 to 12 minutes.

Makes 3 to 4 dozen.

ALMOND MACAROONS

1 16-ounce can almond paste
6 egg whites, unbeaten
2 cups granulated sugar
2 cups confectioners' sugar

In a large bowl, mix the almond paste with two of the egg whites until there are no lumps. Gradually add 1 cup of the granulated sugar and two more egg whites, beating until blended. Add the rest of the granulated sugar, the confectioners' sugar and the last two egg whites, beating until smooth.

Line a cookie sheet with foil paper, shiny side up, grease and flour. Drop cookie dough by the teaspoon on the cookie sheet and bake in a preheated 325° oven for 20 to 25 minutes or until cookies are golden brown.

Cool completely before removing from foil. Can be stored in an airtight container for at least one week.

Makes 3 to 4 dozen

COCONUT REFRIGERATOR COOKIES

1½ cups flour
1 teaspoon baking soda
1 teaspoon salt
1 cup butter or margarine, softened
1 cup brown sugar
1 cup granulated sugar
2 eggs
3 cups rolled oats
½ cup chopped pecans
1½ cups shredded coconut

Sift dry ingredients together.

In large mixing bowl, cream butter and sugars until light and fluffy. Beat in eggs, one at a time, and then add dry ingredients, oats, nuts, and coconut, mixing thoroughly. Divide dough into thirds on 12″ squares of waxed paper, shape in logs, roll in waxed paper and refrigerate up to one week if well wrapped.

Preheat oven to 375°.

Slice ¼″ thick and bake on greased cookie sheet for about 8 minutes.

Makes 5
dozen

GREEK CHRISTMAS COOKIES

1 cup butter, softened
2 cups confectioners' sugar
1 egg yolk
2 cups sifted flour
1 teaspoon cinnamon
½ teaspoon salt
1 teaspoon ground cloves
½ teaspoon nutmeg
1 cup ground (unbleached) almonds
Candied cherries, halved

Preheat oven to 350°.

Cream butter and sugar until light and fluffy. Add egg yolk and remaining ingredients except cherries. Knead well with spoon or hands. Shape small balls with hand dusted in confectioners' sugar. Put on greased cookie sheet approximately 3″ apart. Place half a cherry in center of each. Bake until golden, about 15 minutes. Cool on rack.

Makes 4 dozen

HEALTH COOKIES

1 cup butter or margarine
1½ cups brown sugar, firmly packed
2 eggs
1 Tablespoon vanilla
1 teaspoon cinnamon
1 teaspoon nutmeg
1 cup rolled oats
1 cup whole wheat flour
1 cup wheat germ
1 cup sunflower seeds
2 teaspoons baking powder
½ teaspoon salt

Preheat oven to 350°.

Cream butter and brown sugar. Add remaining ingredients and mix well. Drop by rounded teaspoons on lightly greased cookie sheet.

Bake for 8 to 10 minutes. These are better if not baked too long.

Makes 4 dozen

MICROWAVE NUTTY TOFFEE

2 cups sugar
⅔ cup butter
2 Tablespoons water
1 Tablespoon light corn syrup
1 teaspoon vanilla extract
1 6-ounce package semisweet chocolate morsels
1 cup finely chopped pecans

Combine sugar, butter, water and corn syrup in a deep 3-quart casserole. Microwave at HIGH for 11 to 13½ minutes or until mixture reaches hard crack stage. (Mixture should separate into hard, brittle threads when a small amount is dropped into cold water.)

Stir in vanilla. Pour into an ungreased 15x10x1-inch jellyroll pan, spreading to edges of pan.

Sprinkle chocolate morsels over toffee; let stand 1 minute or until chocolate begins to melt. Spread chocolate over entire candy layer and sprinkle with pecans. Refrigerate until set, and break into pieces. Store in refrigerator.

MICROWAVE MILLIONAIRES

1 14-ounce package caramels
1½ Tablespoons milk
2 cups coarsely chopped pecans
1 12-ounce package semisweet chocolate morsels
½ Tablespoon vegetable shortening

Unwrap caramels and place in a 2-quart casserole. Microwave at HIGH for 1 to 1¼ minutes; stir well with wooden spoon. Add milk to caramels and microwave at HIGH for 1½ to 2 minutes, stirring every 30 seconds. Add pecans and mix well. Drop by teaspoonfuls onto buttered waxed paper. Cool, cover and chill.

Combine chocolate morsels and shortening in a 4-cup glass measure. Microwave at MEDIUM for 3 to 4 minutes or until chocolate is softened; stir well.

Dip caramel centers into chocolate and return to waxed paper.

Store candy in refrigerator.

desserts

CHOCOLATE CHARLOTTE

This elegant dessert can be kept in the freezer up to a month.

2 dozen lady fingers
¼ cup white creme de menthe or rum
16 ounces semi-sweet chocolate
3 Tablespoons instant coffee
½ cup boiling water
6 egg yolks
½ cup granulated sugar
1 teaspoon vanilla
6 egg whites
1½ cups heavy cream, whipped

Split lady fingers but do not separate into individual pieces. Brush flat surfaces with creme de menthe or rum. Line sides of a 9″ spring-form pan with lady fingers, rounded sides against the pan. Separate remaining lady fingers and line bottom of pan, overlapping to fit.

Melt chocolate in top of double boiler, stirring occasionally.

Dissolve coffee in boiling water.

Beat egg yolks at high speed until foamy. Beat in sugar gradually until thick. Reduce speed. Beat in vanilla, coffee and melted chocolate.

Wash beaters. Beat egg whites in large bowl until stiff. Stir about 1 cup of egg whites into chocolate mixture to lighten. Fold chocolate mixture into remaining egg whites. Fold in whipped cream. Pour into lined pan. Freeze until firm. Garnish with chocolate curls and whipped cream. Cover with foil and keep in freezer.

Serves 12 to 16

FABULOUS FRUIT PIZZA

1 17-ounce package refrigerated sugar cookies
8 ounces cream cheese, softened
2 teaspoons vanilla
½ cup granulated sugar
3 to 4 bananas, sliced
4 to 6 peaches sliced (fresh or canned)
2 cups sliced strawberries
Orange glaze
Whipped cream (optional)

Orange Glaze
½ cup granulated sugar
2 Tablespoons cornstarch
Dash of salt
½ cup water
1 cup orange juice

Slice cookies ¼ inch thick and place slices in an oiled pizza pan to form crust. Do not overlap cookies as they will spread during cooking. Bake at 350° for 10 minutes. Remove from oven and cool in pan.

Mix cream cheese, vanilla and sugar and spread over cookie crust. Cover cream cheese mixture with a layer of bananas, a layer of peaches and a layer of strawberries. Any seasonal fruit may be substituted. Cover with orange glaze and refrigerate.

For glaze, combine ingredients in a saucepan and cook over medium heat. Bring to a boil and continue cooking two minutes. Cool.

Cut in wedges and serve with whipped cream, if desired.

Makes 8
servings

BRANDIED PEACH MOUSSE

⅓ cup granulated sugar
2 cups canned peaches, drained
½ cup peach syrup
½ cup brandy
⅛ teaspoon almond extract
1 cup heavy cream

Place all ingredients except cream in blender and blend until smooth.

Whip cream and fold into peach mixture. Pour into a 6 cup mold and freeze until firm.

Cover mold with a towel dipped in hot water for a minute or two, unmold on plate and garnish with peach slices, lemon slices and mint.

Serves 6

LEMON PUDDING

3 egg whites
2 Tablespoons butter, softened
1 cup granulated sugar
Rind of 1 lemon, grated
3 eggs, separated
5 Tablespoons lemon juice
4 Tablespoons flour
1½ cups milk

Beat egg whites until stiff.

Cream butter, sugar and lemon rind with a pinch of salt. Add egg yolks, beat well. Stir in lemon juice, flour and milk. Fold in egg whites. Pour into a buttered, 1 quart baking dish, set in a pan of water and bake at 350° for 45 minutes.

Serves 4

VELVET PUDDING

4 egg yolks, well beaten
½ cup granulated sugar
3 cups milk
1 teaspoon vanilla
⅛ teaspoon salt
1½ Tablespoons gelatin, dissolved in ¼ cup hot water
1 cup heavy cream, whipped

Place egg yolks, sugar, milk, vanilla and salt in a double boiler. Cook about 15 minutes, stirring constantly. Add softened gelatin. Place in refrigerator to cool (approximately 3 hours), stirring occasionally until mixture begins to set. Fold in whipped cream. Pour into a mold and chill until firm.

Serve with additional whipped cream and strawberries.

Serves 6

PINEAPPLE DESSERT

2 cups graham cracker crumbs
½ cup melted butter
½ cup butter
1 cup granulated sugar
3 eggs
1 20-ounce can crushed pineapple, drained
½ pint heavy cream, whipped
1 teaspoon vanilla
2 Tablespoons granulated sugar

Mix cracker crumbs and butter and pat into a 9″ x 12″ glass dish.

Cream butter and sugar thoroughly. Add eggs, beating well after each egg, then beating well after all eggs are added. Spread over crumbs. Spread pineapple over this.

Whip cream stiff, adding vanilla and sugar and spread over pineapple. Top lightly with more crushed cracker crumbs and a maraschino cherry for each piece. Chill 24 hours.

Serves 8

MACAROON SHERBET DESSERT

This is delicious served with Sherry Chocolate Sauce.

2 cups whipped dessert topping
¾ cup chopped walnuts
2 cups macaroon crumbs
1 pint lime sherbet (raspberry sherbet or mint-flavored ice cream may be substituted)

Combine dessert topping, walnuts and macaroon crumbs. Put half of this mixture in a 9″ x 5″ loaf pan. Chill in freezer for ½ hour.

Cover with softened sherbet. Cover with remaining topping mixture. Garnish with maraschino cherries. Freeze until just before serving. Slice.

Serves 6 to 8.

FROZEN PEANUT SQUARES

¼ cup margarine
2 cups vanilla wafer crumbs
½ cup margarine
2 cups unsifted confectioners' sugar
3 eggs
6 ounces chocolate chips, melted
1½ cups coarsely chopped salted peanuts
½ gallon vanilla ice cream

Melt ¼ cup margarine and mix with vanilla wafer crumbs. Pat in 9″ x 13″ pan.

Cream ½ cup margarine, sugar and eggs; stir in melted chocolate and 1 cup nuts. Pour over crust in pan and freeze.

When frozen, top with ice cream and put back in freezer.

Just before serving, sprinkle with remaining ½ cup nuts.

Serves
12 to 15

BANANA SPLIT DESSERT

This is a great recipe for a crowd.

3 cups graham cracker crumbs
3 to 4 bananas
½ gallon Neopolitan ice cream (square carton)
1 cup chopped nuts
1 cup chocolate chips
½ cup butter or margarine
2 cups confectioners' sugar
1½ cups evaporated milk
1 teaspoon vanilla
2 cups whipped topping

Cover the bottom of an 11″ x 15″ pan with 2 cups graham cracker crumbs. Slice bananas crosswise and layer over crust. Slice ice cream into ½ inch thick slices and place over bananas. Sprinkle ice cream with chopped nuts and freeze until firm.

Melt chocolate chips and butter. Stir in confectioners' sugar and evaporated milk. Cook mixture until thick and smooth, stirring constantly. Remove from heat and add vanilla. Cool chocolate mixture and pour over the ice cream. Freeze until firm.

Spread whipped topping over the chocolate layer and top with 1 cup graham cracker crumbs. Store in the freezer. Remove about 10 minutes before serving. Will keep in freezer several weeks.

Serves 25

RASPBERRY CHEESE CAKE

This is best made the day before so it can mellow.

For graham cracker crust:

1½ cups crushed graham crackers
¼ cup sugar
4 Tablespoons soft margarine or butter

Mix together and spread in bottom of 8″, 9″ or 10″ spring form pan.

Bake at 350° for 5 minutes.

In blender or food processor combine:

3 8-ounce packages cream cheese
3 eggs
1 cup sugar
2 teaspoons vanilla
½ teaspoon almond extract

Pour into pan with crust and bake for 35 minutes. Refrigerate for 30 minutes to stop cooking.

Mix together:

2 cups sour cream
3 Tablespoons sugar
1 teaspoon vanilla

Spread over cake and bake for 5 minutes at 350°. Refrigerate until cool.

For topping:

1 10-ounce package frozen raspberries or strawberries
2 Tablespoons sugar
1 Tablespoon cornstarch
Dash of salt

Mix together and cook over medium heat, stirring until thick. Cool and add 1 teaspoon lemon juice. Add topping over sour cream.

Serves 12 to 16

POPCORN CAKE

A fun Christmas cake. Can also be made into popcorn balls.

- 16-ounce package marshmallows
- ½ cup butter
- 11 cups unsalted popcorn
- ½ cup chopped nuts
- ½ cup small gumdrops
- ½ cup ground peppermint candy

Melt marshmallows and butter together in heavy saucepan. Mix in other ingredients. Pack into a buttered tube pan. Cool.

When cool, remove and trim with gumdrops.

To serve, slice like cake.

SUZAN'S PEARS

8 pears
2 cups mincemeat
¼ cup chopped pecans
2 cups white wine
5 good shakes nutmeg
5 good shakes cinnamon
½ cup brown sugar, firmly packed
4 Tablespoons butter

Wash pears, scoop out bottoms and core.

Combine mincemeat and pecans and spoon into pears. Stand pears up in a shallow dish; pour wine over and sprinkle with nutmeg, cinnamon and sugar.

Bake at 350° about 1 hour or until tender. Remove skin and serve with a hard sauce.

Serves 8

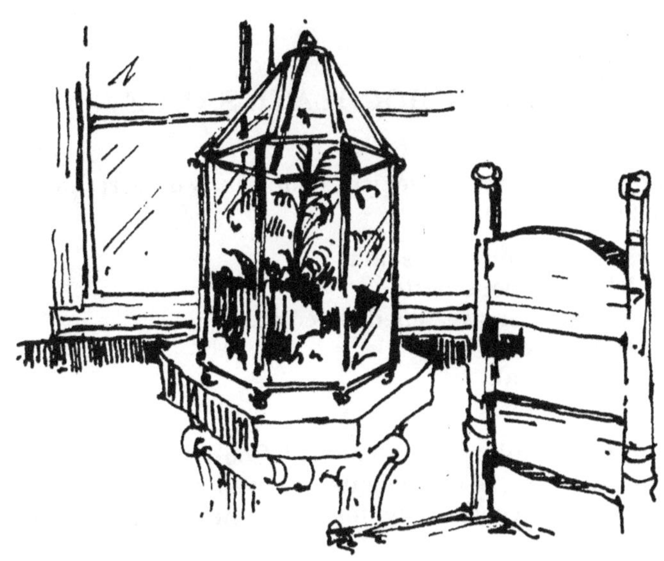

HOT FUDGE SAUCE

1 6-ounce package chocolate chips
¼ cup hot water
1 Tablespoon butter
¼ cup granulated sugar
Dash of salt
1 teaspoon vanilla
¼ cup light Karo syrup

In a small pan, melt chocolate chips with hot water and butter. When melted, add sugar and salt and continue cooking until sugar is dissolved (keep on low heat). Remove from heat and add vanilla and corn syrup. Serve warm.

Makes 1½
cups

SHERRY CHOCOLATE SAUCE

This can be served warm over ice cream or any dessert that calls for a chocolate sauce.

¾ cup granulated sugar
2 Tablespoons butter
2 ounces unsweetened chocolate
½ cup cream
Dash of salt
⅓ cup sherry

In a saucepan, combine all but sherry. Cook over low heat, stirring constantly until ingredients are well blended. Allow to simmer, stirring occasionally, for 6 or 7 minutes. Remove from heat and add sherry.

Makes 2
cups

PINEAPPLE CAKE

2 eggs, beaten
1½ cups sugar
1 20-ounce can crushed pineapple
2 cups flour
1 teaspoon baking soda
½ teaspoon salt
1 teaspoon vanilla

Icing
¾ cup sugar
¼ cup milk
½ cup melted butter
1 cup broken walnuts

Preheat oven to 350°

Mix eggs and sugar well and stir in pineapple and juice.

Sift dry ingredients and add to egg mixture. Add vanilla and mix. Bake in a greased and floured 9 x 13-inch pan at 350°.

For icing, add sugar and milk to melted butter and boil 4 minutes. Stir in walnuts. Let icing cool before pouring over cooled cake.

BUNCH-OF-FRUIT CAKE

3 cups flour
2 cups granulated sugar
3 teaspoons baking powder
1½ teaspoons salt
1¼ cups cooking oil
1 cup crushed pineapple, undrained
1 teaspoon vanilla
1 teaspoon pineapple extract (optional)
3 eggs
2 cups finely chopped apples
1½ cups chopped dates
1⅓ cups flaked coconut
1 cup chopped nuts
1 cup miniature marshmallows

Glaze
1 cup confectioners' sugar
3 to 4 Tablespoons fruit juice or milk

Preheat oven to 325°.

In large bowl, blend first nine ingredients. Beat 3 minutes at medium speed. Stir in remaining ingredients. Pour into greased and floured 10-inch bundt or tube pan. Bake about 1½ hours, until toothpick inserted in center comes out clean. Cool upright in pan 15 minutes; remove from pan and cool completely. Drizzle with glaze.

BUTTERNUT POUNDCAKE

It is very important that this cake be started in a cold oven.

½ pound butter, softened
½ cup shortening
2½ cups sugar
5 large eggs, must be room temperature
1 Tablespoon vanilla
1 Tablespoon butternut flavoring or 1½ teaspoons almond extract and 1½ teaspoons butter flavoring
3 cups sifted all-purpose flour
1¼ teaspoon salt
1 6-ounce can evaporated milk plus enough water to make 1 cup
1 cup drained and chopped maraschino cherries
1 cup chopped walnuts

Cream butter, shortening and sugar. Add eggs, *one at a time,* beating well after each, then add flavoring. Add flour and salt alternately with milk, ending with flour. Mix well. Gently stir in walnuts and cherries by hand, until just mixed. Pour mixture into a greased and floured tube or bundt pan.

Place in cold oven. Bake at 350° for 2 hours. Do not open the oven door during baking time. Remove from pan as soon as it is done. Cool completely on a wire rack, then wrap in plastic wrap and foil. Can be kept in refrigerator up to 4 weeks.

QUEEN'S SPICE CAKE

1 cup margarine, softened
¾ teaspoon cinnamon
1 teaspoon nutmeg
¼ teaspoon cloves
1½ cups granulated sugar
3 large eggs
2½ cups flour
2 teaspoons baking powder
Pinch of salt
1 cup seedless raisins
½ cup milk
⅓ cup orange juice or brandy

Orange Glaze
4 teaspoons orange juice
½ teaspoon vanilla
1 cup sifted confectioners' sugar

Preheat oven to 350°.

Cream margarine, spices and sugar. Beat in eggs, one at a time.

Sift flour, baking powder and salt and stir in raisins. Add alternately with milk and orange juice or brandy to egg mixture. Bake in greased and lightly floured 9-inch tube pan for 1¼ hours. Cool in pan for 10 minutes. Turn out on rack to finish cooling.

For glaze, beat all ingredients until smooth. Spoon over cake.

WALNUT RUM ROLL

2 Tablespoons butter
7 large eggs, separated
1 cup granulated sugar
1 teaspoon baking powder
1 teaspoon rum extract
2 cups ground walnuts
2 Tablespoons confectioners' sugar

Rum Cream Filling
2 cups heavy cream
4 Tablespoons superfine sugar
2 teaspoons rum extract

Preheat oven to 350°.

Butter an 11″ x 15″ x 1″ jelly roll pan and line wax paper across, tucking in corners and letting 2-inch ends overlap. Brush surface of wax paper with butter.

Beat yolks with wire whip; add sugar a little at a time, stirring constantly until thick and pale yellow. Beat in baking powder, rum extract and 1½ cups walnuts.

Beat egg whites until stiff peaks form and gently fold into batter. Spread onto prepared jelly roll pan. Bake 15 to 18 minutes or until puffed. Remove from oven and cool.

Sprinkle surface with confectioners' sugar. Place sheet of wax paper across top of roll; invert and unmold. Peel off wax paper.

To make filling, whip cream until it begins to thicken and form soft peaks; add sugar and rum extract; beat until stiff peaks form. Spread roll with ½ of cream filling and roll up; transfer to serving platter. Top with remaining cream filling and sprinkle with remaining walnuts.

Serves 8 to 10

ARKANSAS BUTTER CAKE

¾ cup butter (not margarine), softened
2½ cups granulated sugar
4 eggs
1 teaspoon vanilla
2½ teaspoons baking powder
2½ cups flour
1 cup milk

Preheat oven to 350°.

Cream butter and sugar, and add eggs one at a time, beating well after each. Add vanilla.

Add baking powder to the flour and blend into the creamed mixture alternately with the milk. Pour into greased and floured tube pan and bake for 50 minutes.

Delicious as is, or may be iced with chocolate icing.

CHOCOLATE CHIP POUND CAKE

1 18½-ounce package German chocolate cake mix
1 3¾-ounce instant chocolate pudding mix
½ cup sour cream
4 eggs
½ cup cooking oil
½ cup warm water
12-ounce package chocolate chips

Preheat oven to 350°.

Mix all ingredients except chocolate chips and beat 3 minutes. Fold in chocolate chips. Bake in greased and floured tube pan for 55 minutes.

BLACK RUSSIAN CHOCOLATE CAKE

1 18½-ounce chocolate cake mix
1 3-ounce package instant pistachio pudding
¾ cup cooking oil
⅔ cup Kahlua
⅓ cup vodka
4 eggs

Icing
2 cups confectioners' sugar
2 heaping Tablespoons cocoa
¼ cup Kahlua
¼ cup vodka

Preheat oven to 350°.

Combine all ingredients and beat for 5 minutes. Pour into a greased and floured tube pan. Bake for 60 minutes, remove from pan and ice.

For icing, mix all ingredients together and spoon over warm cake. Icing should be on the thin side.

RAISIN CAKE

3 cups flour
2 teaspoons baking soda
1½ teaspoons cinnamon
½ teaspoon nutmeg
½ teaspoon salt
¼ teaspoon ground cloves
2 cups granulated sugar
1 cup mayonnaise
⅓ cup milk
2 eggs
3 cups peeled, chopped apples
1 cup raisins
½ cup chopped walnuts

Frosting

4 ounces cream cheese, softened
¼ cup butter or margarine, softened
1 teaspoon vanilla
2 cups confectioners' sugar

Preheat oven to 350°.

Sift dry ingredients together in large mixing bowl. Add mayonnaise, milk and eggs, beating until well blended. Stir in apples, raisins and nuts. Spoon into greased and floured bundt pan and bake for 50 to 60 minutes. When done, turn out, cool and frost.

For frosting, cream the cream cheese and butter. Beat in vanilla and confectioners' sugar, adding a few drops of milk, if necessary, to make a spreading consistency. Garnish with additional chopped nuts.

UPSIDE DOWN GINGERBREAD CAKE

1 14½-ounce gingerbread mix
1¼ cup lukewarm water or pineapple juice
1 egg
Pinch of salt
¾ cup dark seedless raisins
½ cup broken pecans
2 Tablespoons brown sugar
2 Tablespoons butter or margarine
1 8-ounce can pineapple slices or chunks, drained
Sour cream or whipped cream

Preheat oven to 350°.

Combine gingerbread mix, water or juice, egg and salt and mix well. Stir in half the nuts and half the raisins and set aside.

Grease well a large iron skillet or wide heavy pan. Sprinkle remaining nuts and raisins on bottom of pan; dot with butter and brown sugar. Place pineapple pieces on top, evenly distributed. Pour gingerbread mixture over. Bake for 45 minutes. Cool, loosen bottom and invert carefully. Top each piece with sour cream or whipped cream.

Makes 8 to 10
servings

BANANA NUT CAKE

2¼ cups sifted cake flour
1½ teaspoons baking powder
¾ teaspoon baking soda
¾ teaspoon salt
1½ cups firmly packed brown sugar
¾ cup shortening or butter
½ cup granulated sugar
6 Tablespoons plain yogurt
1½ cups very ripe mashed banana
3 eggs
1½ teaspoons vanilla
1 cup chopped nuts
1 cup raisins
6 Tablespoons flour

Preheat oven to 375°.

Grease and flour two 9 x 5 x 3-inch loaf pans.

Sift flour, baking powder, soda and salt into a large bowl. Stir in brown sugar. Add shortening, granulated sugar, yogurt and banana and mix lightly. Beat with mixer for 2 minutes on low, scraping bowl and beaters often. Add eggs and vanilla and continue beating for 1 more minute.

Mix nuts and raisins with 6 tablespoons of flour. Fold into cake batter, mixing well.

Divide batter between prepared pans and bake for 45 minutes to 1 hour.

Cakes freeze well.

MISSISSIPPI MUD CAKE

1¾ cups coffee
¼ cup cup bourbon
5 ounces unsweetened chocolate
1 cup margarine,cut in pieces
2 cups sugar
2 cups flour
1 teaspoon baking soda
⅛ teaspoon salt
2 eggs, lightly beaten
1 teaspoon vanilla

Preheat oven to 275°.

Combine coffee and bourbon in top of double boiler and cook over simmering water for 5 minutes. Add chocolate and margarine. Stir until smooth. Remove pan from heat and add sugar. Cool for 3 minutes. Put into mixer bowl.

Sift flour, soda and salt together and add to chocolate mixture, ½ cup at a time, beating on medium, then beat for 1 additional minute. Add eggs and vanilla and beat until smooth. Pour into a 9″ tube pan, greased and dusted with cocoa.

Bake for 1½ hours.

Serve with sweetened whipped cream flavored with white creme de cacao.

TRULY DIFFERENT CUPCAKES

A glaze is formed on top of cakes during baking so cupcakes don't need frosting.

4 ounces semi-sweet chocolate
1 cup margarine
1½ cups broken nuts
1 cup unsifted all-purpose flour
1¾ cups sugar
1 teaspoon vanilla
4 large eggs, slight beaten

Preheat oven to 325°.

Melt chocolate and margarine together; stir in nuts.

In a separate bowl, mix remaining ingredients. DO NOT BEAT. Add chocolate/nut mixture, stirring carefully. DO NOT BEAT. Spoon into paper-lined muffin tins, filling half full. Bake 30 to 40 minutes. Freezes well.

Makes 2 dozen.

KANSAS PEANUT BUTTER PIE

1 cup granulated sugar
⅓ cup cornstarch
3 egg yolks
Milk for thin paste
2½ cups hot milk
3 heaping Tablespoons crunchy peanut butter
1 9″ baked pie shell

Combine the sugar, cornstarch and egg yolks with enough milk to make a thin paste. Add hot milk and cook until thick. When mixture is thick, not before, add peanut butter and blend. Pour into baked pie shell, top with meringue or whipped cream, sprinkle with crushed fresh peanuts and chill.

APRICOT CRACKER PIE

This is extremely easy!

20 graham crackers, crushed
½ cup sugar
¼ cup melted butter
1 20-ounce can pitted apricots, drained, or
  1 dozen fresh apricots, peeled, cored and sliced.

Topping
1 cup heavy cream
½ teaspoon vanilla extract
½ teaspoon rum extract
2 Tablespoons superfine sugar

Preheat oven to 325°.

Combine cracker crumbs with sugar and butter, mixing well. Divide mixture in half and spread half of mixture in the bottom of a 9″ pie plate to form a crust. Arrange drained apricots on top of crust and top with remaining graham cracker mixture. Bake for 30 minutes.

Serve warm with whipped cream topping. For topping, beat cream until it begins to thicken; stir in remaining ingredients and beat until stiff peaks form.

Peaches, nectarines, and papaya may be substituted for apricots in this recipe. If desired, serve with peach or strawberry ice cream instead of whipped cream.

IMPOSSIBLE PIE

4 eggs
1 cup sugar
2 cups milk
½ cup butter or margarine
½ cup flour
1 teaspoon vanilla
1 cup shredded coconut
¼ to ½ teaspoon nutmeg

Preheat oven to 350°.

Blend all ingredients in blender. Pour into a 10-inch greased pie pan and bake 1 hour until set. DO NOT use smaller pan.

MOLASSES PIE

½ cup brown sugar, lightly packed
5 Tablespoons cornstarch
⅛ teaspoon salt
1½ cups water
½ cup molasses
1 cup raisins
1 teaspoon grated orange rind
Pinch of nutmeg
1 9-inch baked pie shell

Combine sugar, cornstarch and salt in saucepan. Add water gradually, stirring until smooth. Stir in remaining ingredients. Continue cooking over medium heat, stirring constantly until thickened and clear. Remove from heat and cool to lukewarm. Pour filling into baked pie shell. Refrigerate until ready to serve. May be served with whipped cream.

EASY PIE CRUST

1 pound lard
5 cups unsifted flour
1 Tablespoon salt
1 egg
2 teaspoons white vinegar
Water

Put flour and salt in large mixing bowl. Cut in lard until pieces are about the size of a pea. Put egg in a measuring cup and add vinegar. Add enough water to make 1 cup liquid. Stir vigorously. Add to flour mixture and mix by hand. Roll dough into a log shape and cut into 8 equal pieces. Roll each piece into a ball, wrap and freeze until needed. Thaw and roll out for crust.

Yield — 8 single pie crusts.

CONTRIBUTORS

Our sincere thanks and appreciation to all who submitted recipes.

Sr. Ruth Abercrombie
Helene Abraham
Doris Allen
Evelyn Allen
Kay Allen
Marianne Almquist
Jan Alsever
Doris Anderson
Mary Arendt
Kimball Arnold
Bonnie Ashton
Holly Backman
Fleeta Baldwin
Betty Barker
Sandra Barnes
Kay Beachy
Ann Beardsley
Ronnie Berger
Diane Bernene
Sue Bernstein
Mrs. John M. Blair
Taffy Block
Debbie Borland
Marcia Boston
Stuart Bradbury
Lynn Britton
Vicki Budinger
Connie Burke
Ellen Campbell
The Rev. Carl Carlozzi
Linda Carlozzi
Susan Christian
Carolyn Clark
Julie Clark
Linda Clifford
Kathleen Clymer
Kitty Colt
Meredyth Corbett
Felice Coutchie
Catherine Cox
Jane Coy
Elizabeth Culley
Ann Davis
Pearl DeClusin
Mikell Denning
Carol Dennis
Mrs. Fred DeWerth, Jr.
Cynthia Dunn
Joan Dunn
Mrs. Ray Eaton
Mrs. Lloyd Eisele
Cari Ellis
Eleanor Ellis
Pat Fisher
Mrs. Carl Fletcher
Mrs. William French
Mrs. Robert Gallaher
Bonnie Garrison
Cindy Gilbert
Shirley Gimmey
Ann Goldsworthy
Joan Gorczyk
Bev Graham
Sally Griffith
Chuck Hahn
Donna Hahn
Mrs. Jiles Haney
Diana Hayward-Butt
Joni Hegel
Betty Heisley
Dorothy Heitel
Joan Hill
Ruth Holland
Dan Hooper
Barbara Howard
Nadine Huiskamp
Nancy Hume
Barbara Johnson
Mrs. Glenn Johnson
Ruth B. Johnson
Judi Johnston
Carol Jones
Jeanne Jones
Joyce Jones
Suzanne Kapp
Mrs. George King
Connie Kroll
Judith Kunkel
Cindy Langdon
Mary Larkin
David and Martha Lee
Cathie Lemon
Daphne Linn
Mr. and Mrs. Larry Lintner
Kay Lodge
Helen Lowe
Muriel MacCready
Suzan Makaus
Dede Mangum
Gwen Mann

Susan Mark
Helen M. Marty
Florabel Mascarella
Lynn Mitchell
Nancy Mitchell
Lora M. Moore
Gladys Morrison
Kathy Munninger
Shirley Murray
Mary McArthur
Muriel McClellan
Persis McClennen
Eleanor McDaniel
Marvin McNatt
Jean Neal
Rochelle O'Brien
Mary O'Riley
Linda M. Osorio
Elizabeth A. Paddock
Betty Papa
Jeannette Pascal
Mrs. Joseph B. Pennington
Lettie Pickrell
Jane Polacher
Sandra Pollak
Francey Potter
Herman Price
Helen Randolph
Barbara Ransbottom
Robin Rasciner
Patricia Rauscher
Bill Reid
Connie Rodie
Pat Roselle
Elaine Rutledge
Bob Rutherford
Margo Rutherford
Paula Schroeder
Vivian Schwarz
Marion Scoville
Beverly Shaver
Barbara Smelzer
Kathryn Smith
Theodora Smith
Mrs. Ann Smith
Pat Spencer
Mrs. Robert Steward
Judy Stewart
Judy Stoddard
Claire Stone
Anne Sullivan
Roberta Tandler
Nancy Tanita
Linda Thompson
Frances Thorp
Susan Tierney
Margaret Timmerman
Lyn Tinker
Maria Tormey
Gretchen Torrey
Virginia Torrey
Cynthia Tubbs
Barbara Van Arsdale
Mary Ellen Van de Wyngaerde
Linda Vaughan
Brenda Vermeire
Mrs. Jim Watkins
Peggy White
Norma Wilkerson
Anne Wilkins
Doris Wilkinson
Libby Williams
Peggy Wolfe
Ruth Zeluff
June Zittel

INDEX

A

B

C

D

E

F

G

H

I

J

K

L

M

O

P

Q

T

U

V

W

Y

Z

Additional copies may be obtained from:

DESERT POTLUCK COOKBOOK
c/o All Saints' Episcopal Church
6300 North Central Avenue
Phoenix, Arizona 85012

$10.00 per copy plus handling and mailing charges of $1.75 each.

ABOUT THE ARTIST:

DeLOYHT-ARENDT

Mary DeLoyht-Arendt received her A.A. Degree from Columbia College, Columbia, Missouri, and a B.A. Degree, Fine Arts, from the University of Missouri.

Her professional career includes Commercial Artist for Hallmark and American Greeting Cards.

She is a member of the National Society of Arts and Letters, Arizona Artist Guild, Arizona Watercolor Association and 22 x 30 Professional Watercolor Group. Mary has been widely exhibited, receiving numerous awards for her work. Her most recent recognition includes exhibiting with the 1982 National Invitational Watercolor West Exhibit and the Midwest Watercolor Juried Exhibit in West Bend, Wisconsin.

Mary lives in Phoenix, Arizona where she teaches painting in both oil and watercolor.

Mail To:

DESERT POTLUCK COOKBOOK
c/o All Saints' Episcopal Church
6300 North Central Avenue
Phoenix, Arizona 85012

Please send me __________ copies of DESERT POTLUCK at $10.00 per copy. I am including $1.75 each to cover postage and handling. (U.S. Funds only.)

Name ____

Address ____

City/State/Zip _____________________________________

Enclosed is my check or money order in the amount of $______________.
Make checks payable to DESERT POTLUCK.

The proceeds from the sale of this book will be used for Church and Day School projects and programs.

Mail To:

DESERT POTLUCK COOKBOOK
c/o All Saints' Episcopal Church
6300 North Central Avenue
Phoenix, Arizona 85012

Please send me __________ copies of DESERT POTLUCK at $10.00 per copy. I am including $1.75 each to cover postage and handling. (U.S. Funds only.)

Name ____

Address ____

City/State/Zip _____________________________________

Enclosed is my check or money order in the amount of $______________.
Make checks payable to DESERT POTLUCK.

The proceeds from the sale of this book will be used for Church and Day School projects and programs.

Mail To:

DESERT POTLUCK COOKBOOK
c/o All Saints' Episcopal Church
6300 North Central Avenue
Phoenix, Arizona 85012

Please send me __________ copies of DESERT POTLUCK at $10.00 per copy. I am including $1.75 each to cover postage and handling. (U.S. Funds only.)

Name ____

Address ____

City/State/Zip _____________________________________

Enclosed is my check or money order in the amount of $______________.
Make checks payable to DESERT POTLUCK.

The proceeds from the sale of this book will be used for Church and Day School projects and programs.